GRACED WITH WOMANHOOD

A MEMOIR OF THINGS UNSAID

FRANCES PRATT

First published by Ultimate World Publishing 2021
Copyright © 2021 Frances Pratt

ISBN

Paperback: 978-1-922497-42-0
Ebook: 978-1-922497-43-7

Frances Pratt has asserted her rights under the Copyright, Designs and Patents Act 1988 to be identified as the author of this work. The information in this book is based on the author's experiences and opinions. The publisher specifically disclaims responsibility for any adverse consequences which may result from use of the information contained herein. Permission to use information has been sought by the author. Any breaches will be rectified in further editions of the book.

All rights reserved. No part of this publication may be reproduced, stored in or introduced into a retrieval system, or transmitted in any form, or by any means (electronic, mechanical, photocopying, recording or otherwise) without the prior written permission of the author. Any person who does any unauthorised act in relation to this publication may be liable to criminal prosecution and civil claims for damages. Enquiries should be made through the publisher.

Cover design: Ultimate World Publishing
Layout and typesetting: Ultimate World Publishing
Editor: Maria Philip

Ultimate World Publishing
Diamond Creek,
Victoria Australia 3089
www.writeabook.com.au

Dedication

For the magnificent man I created.

Contents

Dedication	iii
Foreword	vii
Introduction	ix
Chapter 1: Beyond Shredding	1
Chapter 2: Unflattering Compulsions	7
Chapter 3: Goodbye Fallopian Tubes	11
Chapter 4: No Prob-Llama	17
Chapter 5: Puppy Love	21
Chapter 6: Raspberry Vomit	25
Chapter 7: My Hourly Rate	37
Chapter 8: The Diamond in the Snail	45
Chapter 9: No Pharos	51
Chapter 10: Life With or Without You	59
Chapter 11: The Good Stuff	69
Chapter 12: I'm Not About Waiting	77
Chapter 13: Miracle #2	87
Chapter 14: My First Sober Breakup	95
Chapter 15: Guaranteed Destruction	103
Part II: For the Love of Womanhood	107
Afterword	119
Further Reading	121
About the Author	125
Acknowledgements	133

Foreword

I do so adore being a woman with all of its grace.

I wish to acknowledge my white privilege, having shelter and food, having conceived and given birth, having access to health care and living in a great community.

Please note the content may be triggering to some of you. If at any time you need to, take a break and come back when you are ready. Trained professionals are available to support you at www.lifeline.org.au. Refer to other services in your area.

No part of this book is intended to be a substitute for professional advice, diagnosis, medical treatment, medication or therapy. Always seek the advice of your physician or qualified mental health provider with any questions you may have regarding any mental health symptom or medical condition. I am not authorised to make recommendations as a substitute for professional advice. Never disregard professional, psychological or medical advice or delay in seeking professional advice or treatment because of something you have read in this book.

Introduction

Imagine the collective stories we hold of our lives up until now. Each story we hear has wonders and joys if we look for them. A story hangs in the air though we cannot see it. They dangle in the universe and drift away without being touched. They are heard and then gone. The heavier they land upon us, the fiercer the energy penetrates ours, the more of them we keep with us. Consciously or not, we take them into our being. Still, they disappear with the constant movement we barely observe as the Earth under all of us gently rolls.

I hold the following stories with love and freedom. I have come to treasure the past sorrows and rewrite much of the influence of their weight for myself. To go to a place where I am capable of this, at this point in my existence, admittedly was not easy or by accident. I sit and simply experience moments of wonder and joy as they come.

CHAPTER 1

Beyond Shredding

Sitting in the sunny lounge with five women I barely knew, I was honestly unaware my neurotic practices would be so intriguing to them. When I started to share, I expected understanding and acceptance. Before that came, I received laughter and animated bewilderment.

I knew as I prepared to speak, it wasn't with pride. I felt a pang of shame and anxiety in my voice. Only once before had I told anyone about my antics. Now both times it elicited this reaction. Both times my confidantes suggested it would make a great book.

I talked about one of my long-standing habits unwittingly, like an admission to ease my nerves. Behind my isolated confession was a bigger picture I hadn't spoken about out loud before. Somewhere in the middle is one that has held a lasting significance.

I once generated a panic attack on a plane headed to Canberra. I was travelling for a work meeting of my nationwide peers. It only took one moment for a thought to arise with total clarity. If I died on the plane, my copious journals would be discovered by my grieving family. Oddly, the dread seemed to me like an appropriate reaction to the situation at the time. The humiliation of someone reading what I had said to myself alone would follow me in whatever afterlife was after my life.

I was perched high above the world and powerless to do anything. My unhelpful brain repeated, "Where the fuck did I leave my journal?"

I had finished my writing at 5.30 a.m. before leaving for the airport. I could not remember the exact moment I put it away. I couldn't even remember what I had written about or how many pages I had filled.

As my blood pumped faster, my pupils dilated and the cabin lights seemed impossibly bright. A familiar gentle squeeze at my temples quickly tightened. I avoided speaking to my colleague who was oblivious at my side.

With some slow breathing, loud music pumped through my headphones and a weak cup of sweet tea, I convinced myself I must have put it back in its usual hiding spot. It lived in between a pile of old books, on an uninteresting shelf, in an unused room.

By the time we landed, I was thinking enough to rationalise, based on the data I knew, I would be unlikely to die today. Plane or no plane.

When we landed, I urgently texted one of my best friends. I asked her if I should perish today or any other day, would she go to my house and destroy any notebooks and journals she could find? This would be my dying wish. In return, she asked me to do the same with her vibrator.

She was no more aware of the contents than anyone else, better she read them though than anyone else, not to say she would even care. As a woman who owns a rubber dick, she would understand discretion.

I could have taken this incident as a clue that I wasn't really at peace with myself or my life. Instead, I took it as a red flag to act with the strictest of caution with my writing from now on given the severity and lack of discipline.

My journaling was at the point where I would have three to six notebooks on the go. At least one in my handbag, one at my desk and one in the car. Usually, there'd be one at my bedside table and one at work for less significant matters.

The notebooks at work and in the car would regularly be removed. They held an additional risk by being out of the house.

What if one fell out when I opened the car door?

Maybe I wouldn't see it, and it would sit in the gutter of a car park.

Someone might notice the beautiful cover (they all have a beautiful cover).

Then, the dread of all dread, they pick it up and read it.

Although it doesn't have my name or any other names or identifying details mentioned anywhere, they may recognise it's me.

Imagine if it just happened I went to primary school with this imagined perpetrator or I had sacked this nosy person from their job or they were one of my ex-husbands.

What had grown from an innocuous start now left me with a compulsive need to be surrounded by the magical places to shift out of my head. I needed desperately to manifest into the world through ink on paper. At the same time taking a gamble that no one would ever, ever hear my real voice.

Enter the shredder. I have destroyed my pages by soaking them in soapy water and burning them in fireplaces and fire pots. I've incinerated them in glass jars that shattered in the heat and cardboard boxes that unsurprisingly also burnt in a mess of ashes and a mass of smoke I extinguished with my garden house.

In a saner moment, it occurred to me the shredding machine at work would be a better option. I would risk taking the contents to the office, but I figured if I paid enough care and attention, I could destroy them unseen.

Off I go one morning with my pages ripped from every current journal. I stowed them neatly in a sealed bag, inside a book, inside a carry bag.

I waited until lunchtime for there to be fewer conversations in the shredding room and ducked in to purge myself. All went to plan. In less than ten minutes, the job was done. Back to my desk, grabbed some food and off for a walk in the sun.

I got halfway down the block, and it hit me anyone with some tape and a little patience could undo my handiwork. We've all seen it on TV. The persistent detective was waist-deep in fine strips of paper. They make it look easy. It can't be hard to stick shredded paper back together.

Too panicked to eat, I headed straight back to the office. When I removed the lid from the machine, I recognised my identifiable paper. Thank goodness it was still there. I shoved it into my bag, within a book, within a bag. I minded it dutifully until driving home when I stopped to discard it in an anonymous rubbish bin.

Beyond Shredding

People have obsessions, and addictions can sneak up slowly. I didn't see this one until I read it in the expressions of those unknown companions over lattes and carrot cake. What I didn't notice at first was the shift in its power over me by the simple act of my speaking aloud.

"What on earth is in your journals?" one of my unfamiliar new friends had asked.

How tantalising I must have made it sound. What horrors and torrid secrets or titillating gossip must they contain? In truth, there is a bit, I suppose. I will get to it shortly. Mainly though, in the faces of my new fast friends, I saw how naked and terrified I felt at the notion of being outed as a different version of me to the one I assumed they saw.

Speaking of my lunacy was the first time I showed this secret and shady side of myself.

Here I am then. Me, the shredder I purchased at Officeworks for $99 and the seven journals I have on the go.

CHAPTER 2

Unflattering Compulsions

Some say life is short. It didn't seem that way to me nearing my 40th birthday. In response to circumstances or the realisations of age, I was toying with the notion I'd had enough. I wondered if there might be a better place I could be. Where I didn't know, I figured it didn't matter.

I had tackled early life being as good as possible. A good girl by nurture rather than nature. A common symptom of girlhood. I was happy to show the world my perfection. My foibles and misdemeanours I kept to myself. Somewhere along the way, it became hard to keep hidden the parts of me that were not so perfect.

I have tried to speak to professionals but found myself putting on the usual good girl performance. It was important they liked me, and to see at worst, I had made a few entirely understandable and forgivable dubious choices. I have turned to the odd trusted friend and family member over the years. Carefully, I ensured no one knew much at all.

Who else could I tell the whole and complete truth to but myself? Not that it was ever the whole and absolute truth. Finding truth by myself never really happened.

I have written diaries and journals since as early as I remember. About five years ago I picked up a book at random by Julia Cameron, titled *The Artist's Way*. I was not looking for inspiration that day, but it found me just the same.

The author's encouragement to write an unfettered daily trail of the inner monologue was all the approval I needed. From then on, I started having more and more conversations with myself.

The recommendation was well-intentioned. Well-designed to give the writer personal freedom. To let out the unconscious wanderings of the nights' slumber and get on with living through the day. I loved it. How brilliant. What a terrific idea. It sounded exactly what would give me back some room in my head.

My mind had been thick and messy. It felt heavy and clogged. If I could shift some weight, there would be space for pandas and rainbows and the world of wonder and beauty I was convinced was out there. I hoped to remember the grocery list at the very least.

The problem is, just like sex, booze, food, TV and shopping that at times have become an addict's crutch of escapism for me, Julia's well-meaning suggestion provided the same instant relief as all the others.

Before I knew it, I was stuck in a circuit of grief, shame and emotional triggers. As I wrote stuff came up, and, without releasing it beyond a two-dimensional page, its potency continued to grow. I always feared exposure by daring to put myself authentically into the world, even privately on paper.

Looking back at the history I've carried, I see an earlier moment where this compulsion began. Writing has always been a special joy for me. I treasure my coveted Penmanship Award bestowed upon me in grade six.

As my schooling moved on, the short stories and poems of fantasy worlds soon evolved into four and five thousand-word essays on corporation law and quantitative methods.

I completed my Bachelor of Commerce degree in my hometown, at the only university in the state. By the time I went on to complete my Graduate Diploma in Chartered Accounting, I was well and truly over the art of creative writing.

The preoccupation and hours absorbed with journaling encroached on my daily routines. I was unable to escape the compulsion to shoo out my buzzing thoughts on those pages.

A domestic violence counsellor I saw once mentioned she had some clients who madly journaled to make sense of their traumatic situations. They tried to organise the chaos and find a solution - anything not to endure the terror of leaving an abusive relationship.

I decided she wasn't talking about me. She just mentioned this out of interest. My process was helpful. I was one paragraph away from finding the answer. I knew it was in my head and I needed to write it down in front of me.

The content of my daily prose varied. Some days it lulled me into a passive submission with the flow of a carefully selected pen against the perfectly spaced lines. It would rest in a beautifully bound notebook, with an inspiring quote or pretty artwork adorning the cover.

Other days I rile myself into anger, self-hatred and despair. It's always a gamble whenever I sit down. I don't know which way it's going to flow. It is worth the risk of the latter to experience the former.

If you agree the past only exists in the conversations of the present, then regularly writing pulls things forward in time. The mind and body don't experience time in the linear way we are taught. In my journals, I get to live in yesterday or last year or that time when I was seven and fell from a giant horse.

The rational partner to my journaling is research. In my mind, there must be an expert who's already nutted this out. They can explain the tools I need to decipher this mess. I can catalogue the problems, develop milestone goals and fix everything.

My pile of half-filled notebooks is rivalled only by the stack of books I am part way through reading. There's also the multitude of eBooks and audiobooks that take up less space on my shelves. I just haven't found the exact one yet, but I know it's out there. It could be in the memoir I am reading about a holocaust survivor or the field notes of a university professor. Unlike the illustrious receptacles for my scribbles, these books hold the wisdom that will soon set me free. It turns out wisdom and research might not be the same thing. Just knowing how things are doesn't give you access to the answers.

I recently discovered that the Japanese have a special word – *tsundoku* –- buying books and not reading them, letting them pile up unread, scattered on shelves or nightstands. In my four years of studying the language at high school, I hadn't unearthed that one. What I did get was the first prize in a statewide competition for a visual display I made with felt and coloured pens. From that point onwards, my teacher was so proud the honour had gone to one of her students I pretty much coasted until I finished in grade ten. Today I don't have much beyond ichi, ni, san, yon, go.

CHAPTER 3

Goodbye Fallopian Tubes

I am usually the tallest woman in a room at 181 centimetres. That is obvious. Less obvious is how I wondered if just maybe I could be the smartest, the skinniest, the one in charge, the prettiest, the fastest, the best dressed, the cleanest and the sexiest person in the room. If not, it meant I had work to do.

I imagined I had won some of my contests, usually with people who had no idea they were playing against me. Whether it was the only grade nine girl to have a boyfriend with a job and a car, being head prefect, making the dean's honour roll or being the youngest ever State CEO of my organisation in the country.

One thing time has revealed to me is lots of women wage this struggle with competing to be enough. There is a range of costs for this way of being. Striving to be good enough by being a good girl, cool enough to win imaginary competitions.

It was quite a thing to discover a whole array of physical symptoms can manifest in the body because of the way we are in the world. I accepted the simple idea that thoughts can really make me sick. That took a while to sink in. How is it I found this notion so damned hard to grasp? I would dare to say I did know. I just didn't take any notice. Why is it not the most obvious thing in the world?

Whether suffering from pain emotionally or it radiates to us in our bodies, it is all the same thing. By separating the two, we run a dangerous risk of boxing our conceptions of ways out of misery. I am no stranger to the quest for an answer. I have on staff a counsellor, a caseworker, a social worker, a psychologist, a psychiatrist, a claims manager, an exercise physiologist, a chiropractor, massage therapist, an occupational therapist and a professional coach. I should add in my hairdresser and dentist who are both highly experienced at providing emotional support. I almost forgot my personal trainer, my biomedical practitioner, my naturopath and my reiki healer.

I have collected these people along with my books and journals and share with them bits and pieces as we work together over the months and years.

You might now imagine how my fortune is dwindling, and my head is so darn full. The energy this busy seeking generates needs an exhaust hole.

In my searching, I have had great success. If you look hard enough, you will see evidence to support almost any supposing. In this, I feel a victor. I knew it. There's definitely something wrong with me. So many things are wrong with me.

I won't claim to share any secrets for healing. I can't point to cures for my various conditions although many have been offered to me.

To give you a feel for what I'm talking about I'll list out a few of the "problems" I'm working with here. For starters, clinical anxiety and depression. Okay, millions of people have that going on. We hear a lot about it today. Add in some complex PTSD, and type 2 bipolar disorder and things seem a little more challenging. I wonder how that all happened? Might need to think about it but nutting it out is totally doable.

What about the fibromyalgia which causes or was the cause of chronic fatigue? Two for the price of one. Persistent disordered eating. Sounds nasty but is possibly the most common one yet. Alcoholism. What is that really anyway? Let's not forget arthritis in my lower spine. The newest of the bunch is severe endometriosis, recently discovered. I'm rather proud of finding it too.

I went in for a rub down from my physio, and when it made the pain worse, I went for a bone scan, MRI and X-rays. Then it turned out both the physio and my GP missed the massive growths on my ovaries when the results came back. It was a co-incidental appointment with a rheumatologist for the fibromyalgia who casually asked when I was having the masses removed. Holy cow, what did you say?

I've seen too much to doubt the constant presence of synchronicity. So, however convoluted the process of detection, I got on the table and went under the knife.

When my gynecologist spoke to me after the surgery, it was to share the great news that she'd found my pelvic cavity was "obliterated" with endometrial cells. She took my poor mangled fallopian tubes out, chopped at my ovaries and cut out the masses, scrapped and washed out the lining and freed my uterus from the suffocating cells that had pulled it to one side and left it deformed.

I was too groggy to remember this news in the recovery room, and apparently, I responded very politely. Despite this news, I had been lovely. Believing I was fine, the doctor left for the day and I lay in the hospital bed all night wondering what had happened. Should I be worried? Wait, I'm already worried. Was I barren now? Was I headed for menopause? Was it something... worse?

Sometime around 3 a.m., the aches, cold room and sad thoughts got all a bit much. I decided I needed pharmaceutical intervention. I had surrendered my stash on admission, so I had to find a nurse. Relieving me, the nurse dished out the medication I requested, from my own supply. Five minutes later she flapped back into the room and declared I shouldn't have had that. She rang the head of the hospital and he was on his way up.

Really? Now what?

This was when I made another little discovery. I had been taking a drug for anxiety and as it turned out moonlights as a pretty good pain killer. The extremely serious doctor didn't want to see me self-medicating. I had been for years. I promised to check again with my psychiatrist, knowing full well I was fine.

When the specialist came to my room in the morning, I was pleasant to her when she puzzled over my questions. I'd already been informed apparently.

Finding the endometriosis was an answer to a lifelong source of misery. The doctor could not believe I hadn't sought help before now. I only did now by accident. I thought all women suffered from hormones. Part of the deal.

So no more children without IVF. I'll need to take progesterone to manage the growth of the cells into the future and a gold star for being such a lovely patient. Barely conscious and still such a good girl.

Goodbye Fallopian Tubes

When I went back for my follow-up appointment, the doctor showed me 50 colour photos of the damage and her handiwork. Her assistant had been amazed, she said. There it was. Proof. Something was actually wrong with me.

It's hard to take photos of mental illness with such clarity.

CHAPTER 4

No Prob-Llama

Wellness appears to be a relatively newish concept we now believe should be our highest aspiration. Generations create a focus for our endeavours driven from, let's face it, people who aim to financially gain from our insecurities. In my years, I have witnessed smoking and drinking both viewed as the norm. I've seen a billion delicious sugary treats paraded at every turn and then the emergence of diet and weight loss culture in abundance, now demonised.

When I was younger, I was pretty thin. One of my only memories from my time spent with my aloof grandfather was he called me "Skinny Winnie". In primary school, my weight reduced even further. Then my tonsils were removed. As I understand it now no one really knows what they do anyway, but it was proposed this would help. A superfluous little organ leftover from evolution or an integral part of our physiology, who knows?

Anyhow, the timeline tracks my throat no longer being constantly infected led to the rekindling of my love for my mother's homemade sponge cakes, sausage rolls and caramel slices. Along with all the other masterful foods mum lovingly made. My shape changed, and so did my sense of place in the world now I took up more space in it.

Mum was acutely aware of the challenges young ladies are subject to in society and, while maintaining her baking, took me off to a swimming club twice a week. Four hours of black line tedium in a failed attempt to shift my extra softness. Squeezing on Speedos and flopping into a pool full of trim and fit peers was at the time, not all that helpful. My coach, a well-seasoned man, commented to Mum as a matter-of-fact being a bigger girl was impeding my performance. Make no mistake, my mum loves me with more generosity than anyone I know. I know her intentions were pure and her subconscious soaked in our western diet culture at the time.

With the eventual and welcome end of my chlorine-soaked torture I had learned the then touted key lesson of calories in and calories out. This was a formula. Something to be researched, scheduled and recorded, so a food journal was just the thing.

I don't know if you've ever gone down the path of tracking food intake; some of you might be doing it right now. It has become a standard practice for dietitians and wellness gurus the planet over. At 11, however, the strictness I employed to sustain this habit was a little obsessive upon reflection. I recall my first diary was an insert from the life-changing *Dolly* magazine. Sleek and filled with barely clad women in their late teens, this new Bible was precisely the motivation this dumpy, extremely tall girl needed.

When I measured myself for the first time, as was instructed in my new how-to be a woman guide, I realised I was nothing like these ever so unreal and uncommon beauties rarely seen in my town. Whether or not those images were realistic was irrelevant now. There was a cheerfully snide high school girl who shared my bus ride and constantly teased my weight. Standing head and shoulders above everyone else I was an obvious and easy target.

So back to grade six and my very first diet. The first thing I eliminated from my world was chocolate. I figured an entire ban would be the best way to go. All or nothing. I think of my 11-year-old son and the ice creams and hot chips we now share and wonder what I'd do if he started measuring every morsel he put in his gob and even recorded his outgoings with such dedication as I did. Maybe like me he would do it secretly and not tell a living soul, hiding the diary.

These glorious pages of the magazines were also filled with exercise routines demonstrated in full-colour photos with bikini wearing babes doing lunges on a beach.

Now I've mentioned my height, but I haven't mentioned I was the first girl in my primary school year to become a woman. Don't panic, I don't mean in the back of the car, that was a couple of years away. I, of course, mean my hormonal changes. What a hell of a time I had with it. I'll spare you the details, but the pain and heaviness were off the charts. Not that I understood that because we don't talk about such private things.

My headmistress called me into her office because mum had spoken to her in case of any potential embarrassing accidents. The principal said to me it was such an honour, and I was very special. So I won that prize too. Then she said I wasn't to talk about it with other girls because they had their own journey to take. The early feminist in me wants to go back and ask, "How we will be there for each other, how will we trust and share and grow through all the things life will throw at us, if we can't even talk about this of all womanly things."

I see for myself now how I could be my age and not realise I was riddled with the chronic endometriosis for one thing. When my gynaecologist questioned the absence of severe symptoms I was puzzled until she listed them all. I replied I thought they were just normal. Normal for who I wonder? What's normal anyway?

Isn't it an interesting question? How many times do we let things slide under the guise of normal? It's normal to worry all the time because there's so much to worry about. It's normal to be beyond exhausted at the end of every day because you need to do everything perfectly no matter the drain. It's not normal to be free from worry because you must be missing the point. It's normal to be obsessed with food and weight because we need ourselves to look a certain shape and size. It's normal to drink all the time – it's expected really. The drive to achieve all the things in life will bring happiness. The elusive state right up there with wellness, happiness.

CHAPTER 5

Puppy Love

Many of the actions I was taking were heartbreakingly hard and in the name of eventual happiness. The Dalai Lama is known to have said: "The only responsibility we have is the pursuit of happiness." Great in essence, I saw a few problems.

When I was at university, I found myself married and saving for my first house, living in a complex of tiny units with my new husband. I worked full time at a chartered accounting firm, studying a three-quarter load of coursework and working three nights a week selling a party plan clothing line to ladies as they drank bubbles and gossiped. My upline distributor wrote a piece about my workload in the national newsletter. My embarrassment at the unsolicited fame was coupled with quiet confidence. I knew how to get shit done. Not content with giving my all to a single goal, my dreams all needed to be reached ASAP.

When I had the house of my dreams, new car and my killer wardrobe to show off my soon to be fabulous body I would be my happiest. I would wear my fabulous clothes while doing my new job in management having been top of the class at uni. I did manage to manifest all those ambitions into existence. As soon as they appeared to me, I was on to the next thing.

I went as high as I could go career-wise in the accounting firm, being promoted at every six-month review cycle, finished my degree and then more postgraduate studies. I had my gorgeous home which looked like a dolls house from the street. I had saved the $5,000 deposit and bought the dream at 20. With habits like these ingrained I was hardly going to sit down now and take a rest. Well, I did try. The trouble was when I was forced to spend time with my then husband, I realised I didn't even like him.

He worked shift work at a local supermarket chain stacking shelves from 4 a.m. We started going out when I was 14 years old. And yes, he was the one in whose car I found the other type of womanhood. He was convenient I would probably say. Throughout our ten-year relationship, he was very handy. Having a car and money was very liberating for a teenage girl desperate to grow up as quickly as possible. The first seven years we were together we both lived with our respective parents.

In the first years of our relationship, I got to see him for some time on some weekends between study, work and sport. This worked for me. We didn't really have much in common beyond our hormones and sharing a drive or a movie together. So, when I had space at the finish line of my race to all those dreams, I found nothing there with him.

Puppy Love

I had sprinted ahead into adulthood and my career, while he was still unpacking bananas. I financially supported him to take on an apprenticeship thinking I could fix him up a bit and that would help. Only to see him be even less motivated and more miserable about life.

I was already planning my next big step and it hit me, he just wouldn't do as a father to my children. His job was done. Just like that, I emotionally checked out. I couldn't recall if I ever checked in. I had thought I was in love, of course I did.

We had a fairy tale wedding at the estate home my mother, my grandmother and her mother grew up in after migrating from England. It was in a marquee by a pond in an English rose garden with the homestead in the background. I wore a blush pink coloured dress custom-made by a designer in the stylish fashion district of Brunswick Melbourne. We had a fabulous girls trip to the big smoke, fabulous after the overnight vomit-inducing ferry crossing.

As I walked down the church aisle on my dad's arm at all of 19, one of my cap sleeves fell off. Mum jumped up and ran down the aisle to me to attend to the slippage. Now I wonder what might have happened if she grabbed my arm, and we'd hurried out the door. It was a beautiful summer day and I remember fondly the love and generosity of my family and friends. But not much of my husband. Funny that.

I was never really sure about him. Even on a good day. I would break up with him time and time again. I took down all the cards and teddies and love heart boxes of chocolates and jewellery and swear I was done. It never lasted long.

Six months or so after our final breakup he started dating someone who had actually been a few grades younger than me at high school. I had been pretty recognisable at school not only by my height but also the extracurricular activities meant I knew most of the population. Apparently, she was curious about me, her lawyer said after she was issued with a restraining order on my behalf. She worked a few blocks from my house so the five-kilometre radius ban meant she couldn't go to work for a year.

It had been a bit like a movie and annoying before it got intense. The phone calls to work traced by the police and sitting in her car outside my office and house and following me when I drove, became less and less amusing and more and more concerning. My ex-husband phoned after it was all over to reassure me she was harmless, and he confided she was even weirder than me. Guess he ranked the female race into levels of weirdness.

Before we were engaged I planned to go away to a different city and university campus. I had enrolled and done the orientation of the residential buildings. Life had another plan for me. How grown-up I was, convinced if I did all the things grown-ups do and seemed to want me to do, then I'll grow up with all the wisdom I'll ever need.

CHAPTER 6

Raspberry Vomit

Six years ago, I finished my last full-time job I had. I spent the seven years before working for a very large charity organisation. It was an absolutely amazing role for a benevolent cause. I worked with literally hundreds of dedicated volunteers and staff. They endlessly toiled to feed and home members of their local communities, across the country and for that matter, the world.

My place was supporting the work and it was extremely fulfilling to me personally. I remember the sense of satisfaction on a daily basis, jumping out of bed and working day and night when necessary.

Having previously worked in the corporate sector, my move to the social services had been a big eye-opener. From day one I met fascinating people some of whom are my very best friends to this day. When I saw people on their own or in families struggling to make ends meet every day, the life I had lived took on a whole new meaning to me.

My nuclear family is made up of Mum, Dad and my brother who was 12 months younger than me. My childhood was spread between our seven-acre hobby farm outside a small country town and our family shack at a small beach town.

As an adult I identify more with growing up on the sun-drenched coastline covered in salt and sand. I see mum taking my brother and me to the shoreline across the road every morning, so we wouldn't wake anyone else up with our noise. I don't actually recall being very noisy. When I was born my dad was a milkman, so he worked shift hours. It was crucial we didn't interrupt his rest and being quiet was a habit established early.

Often mistaken as twins, my brother and I were very close and played together most of the time. We would be out racing a billy cart down the rolling paddocks or jumping in our freezing cold pool all year round. I grew up in an island state as far south as is inhabitable. Braving those icy waters on the short winter's days in our peanut-shaped pool or in the surf at the shack were our favourite times back then.

On the farm, we had pigs and sheep. We saw the tails drop off the lambs and the pigs scorched in boiling water after they'd been slaughtered. The story goes Mum received a concerned phone call from my primary school teacher after I'd recounted these incidents in class.

My brother was given his first motorbike one Christmas morning. His pile of individually wrapped presents from Santa had been notably smaller than mine and his disappointment was obvious. It wasn't until we saw Dad buzzing around in the paddock on a red Honda XL100 that he regained his excitement. My brother dinked me around the paddocks for hours that day and many, many more days we spent during our adolescence in the bushland near the shack. The bike is still in the shed. It was passed down to me after my brother outgrew it. He outgrew a lot of things, finally reaching 6 foot 8.

Those bush tracks are where he and I learned to drive. Dad would take us out in his Land Cruiser and set us on his knee until we were old enough to touch the pedals. Then he put us in every vehicle he had. One of Dad's favourite pastimes is buying and selling used vehicles, so they were quite a few. I remember running over a roundabout ever so slightly in a Hiace van and getting a pretty good telling off as only a dad can do.

When it came to the licence test I qualified as a resident of the seaside town. I popped into the local cop shop. A slightly disinterested older policeman asked me questions as we sat in the car park at the station. Then we took a drive around the block. He knew us all of course and being my father's daughter was enough street cred to pass. When I went for the test for my motorboat licence the story was rather similar. Although this time Mum accompanied me armed with freshly caught and cooked crayfish. The older gentleman in the makeshift marine department office on the wharf was more than obliging. I had incorrectly circled a couple of answers, and he gently nudged me in a different direction as we worked through the standard paper test together. I still get confused about which one is the port side.

Dad had a few different jobs over the years moving on from the milk run into real estate briefly and cray fishing. He owned a bus company and then went into the building and construction industry. I grew up knowing my dad could do and build absolutely anything. A trait my brother now too possesses. My parents had traditional male and female roles. My mum dreamed of having children and tending home and her husband. She worked over the years in the pancake shop they owned in the city, the milk bar in the country town, using her skills in horticulture, running cafes and gift stores, delighting endless customers with her thoughtful service. Mum also worked with Dad at the bus company and my brother and me spent time after school hanging around at the depot.

We had a big part of our identity attached to that little farm property perched on the hill surrounded by fields of veggies and livestock, over a hundred rose plants and our beloved pool.

During my high school years, we moved into a suburban house with four rooms and a backyard big enough to subdivide and make money. By then my brother and I were heavily into basketball. I studied around the clock and dated husband #1, so I didn't spend a lot of time in that home.

My memories of that house are dark and lonely despite all my doings I was busy getting up to. I had a close friend who was one of my brother's sporting mates. He was in many of my classes. He was sweet and funny, athletic and doted on me. Apart from my brother and my boyfriend, my other friendships weren't much comfort to me. I found girls my age a little tedious in truth because they didn't seem to share my drive for achievement. I tried all the girly parts of growing up. I learned to care about style, celebrity and in-school social order. I accepted it as part of a girl's life and like everything else made sure I was pretty good at it.

When I was 13, Mum and I went to our local country show. I looked forward to it every year, saving pocket money to go nuts on the rides and show bags. I also loved visiting the cuteness of the animal competitions, the kittens, lambs and coloured ducklings in the petting zoo. While admiring these beautiful critters, an older woman with glorious grey curls, dressed immaculately and totally out of place sidled up to me. I was looking pretty smart myself I guess as part of the annual ritual involved a new outfit. I would hope for a fine day, so I could wear something purchased from the new summer collections but in mid-spring it was more likely than not to be cold and raining.

Raspberry Vomit

Her voice was unusually raspy, and she spoke with an elegance. She was scouting for pageant contestants and I fitted her criteria. Mum was proud and I was curious, so we eventually became involved. This huge pageantry ordeal is no longer run, but in the 1990s it was a big deal. As a contestant, I was tasked with fundraising for the nominated charity, and we had PR events to attend across the year. It was at this point I discovered how competitive mum was as well.

We planned and executed event after event. Raffle tickets were sold in pubs I was too young to be in but was anyway, market stalls, cake stands and a huge spit roast for all the neighbours at the shack. That night we reached a sizable tally from the games and silent auction.

Mum took me to visit several sites operated by the charity and the whole experience was educational for a young lady.

Then came the big night. What a giant magnificent occasion for a 13-year-old. I had an electric blue velvet dress made to highlight my early adolescent features. The hem was scalloped above the knees in front and mid-calf at the back. My hair was curled and pinned and sprayed. My face plastered and my first pair of heels wedged on.

We had to parade on the stage and undergo an interview with the MC. I think we had to dance but that could just be a confused memory. Prior to the evening, we were judged by a panel who were there on the night as we were put through our final paces. Did I mention at this stage I had braces?

While we were waiting backstage my loyal friend who scouted me out at the show that day, snuck up to mum and me. She wanted to prepare me, to be ready to accept the prize, as she heard I had won.

Alas, I had not. I can only imagine my confused and disappointed face at the announcement standing on the stage a good 30 centimetres taller than everyone else. Maybe it's good to learn these lessons of disappointment young.

Mum enrolled me in a modelling course and a whole new side of life opened up in a class with eight 13-year-old girls. We were taught how to walk, dress, make ourselves up, how to exercise and skin care regimes. We had professional photos done and trying to find an appropriate yet not too sexy look at the age of 13 was tricky. We had a graduation and a formal parade working with professional models.

The event was in the cabaret room at the local casino, where I later worked as a server while at university. On the night we were dressed by a local boutique and sent out to work the runway. Backstage one of the pros handed me a packet of band-aids. Apparently my nips were responding to the cold dressing room, and I was in danger of humiliation. She was kind of laughing at me, still it was a lifesaving gesture.

Our achievements in the course were rated, another competition to win. Of course, I attained the highest distinction in the class. I was proud at the time. The best thing is now I rock taking selfies because I can get the angles right.

I did a few paid modeling jobs. Once again for the casino. A TV commercial where I was cackling with laughter winning on a pokie machine. Oh, the shame now. There were some runway shows and a few private showings for designers and local retail outlets. It was so excruciating getting it all right, I struggled how to handle the men who were more interested in finding out what was under the clothes. Anyhow, I figured out I was no Heidi Klum, so I drifted back to study and concentrated all my spare time on ratcheting up my basketball career. Identified young to have the right stuff. In college, I was accepted into an athlete development program. You would not have found me anywhere other than the library or the gym.

Raspberry Vomit

The team was awesome and enjoyed the competition. We took a trip to Canberra for a tournament and spent time at the Australian Institute of Sport. All the other girls got to go home with the cool girls from our rival team and I got lumped with the guy from the men's team. He wouldn't speak to me and so his dad took the lead. He and I went off to a rugby game on the Sunday, league or union I have no idea. He spent three hours explaining the rules and I had visions of the other girls talking about boys and watching movies with popcorn.

The friend of my brother I was close to in high school was also on the Canberra trip. We trained together and we watched each other play. While we were away, he successfully got me home after I'd gotten drunk for the second time ever on vodka and raspberry. It was a very colourful display for later in the night.

In the three or so years of my friendship with him, I never noticed he didn't have any other girlfriends. It turned out I had myself a part-time platonic boyfriend. I don't remember actually thinking it at the time. If I think of it now, I guess he probably was.

We hung out a lot with other people at basketball games including with my brother. He took the same elective classes, became a fellow school executive and helped me secure my first job with him at McDonald's. He even helped cover for me on my first day on the job when I was so nervous and I forgot to put on the hand brake in my little red Pulsar Q hatchback with shiny alloy wheels I'd been given for my 17th birthday. It rolled down the sloped car park, over a garden bed and came to a stop lodged sideways across the drive through. Mercy of all mercies it didn't hit anyone.

He was my date to our grade ten leavers dinner and then came to the same college. I don't have any memory of feeling attracted to him. In truth, he felt like the brother I was so familiar having around. Turns out he didn't see me as the sister he never had. I didn't have close girlfriends to caution me and no one I would trust to talk about such things. My family loved him and when he would join in family events I wondered if they secretly hoped I'd choose him over my older guy, who they mockingly called "Reggie the Veggie". They barely tolerated him in the knowledge I'd soon outgrow him.

The naivety of youth hey. I'm sure I must have seen his crush on me, but he was a comfort, a reliable companion and fun to be around. I was busy getting on with all my plans and he was always close by to bring some comfort of friendship. Right up until one day I came home after a date with my boyfriend and the key was missing from its high-tech hiding spot inside a fake rock on our porch. When I peered through the window, I saw a shape I recognised peering back at us. Unable to be angry but curious as to the situation I calmly tried to lure him outside. I wondered what could be up for him to be stowed away in our house. Had he had a fight with his parents? Was he unwell or did he need to see me? He eventually opened the door and scurried out past us at speed. He sprinted up the road. Never saying a word.

I later found out he'd known where the key was from coming home from school with my brother and I. He'd had easy access to my private world. He would visit my bedroom and look through my things. My precious journals in their hiding places were unsafe from his curious eyes. I'll never understand why neither my boyfriend nor I told my parents or even my brother. I wanted so desperately to trust him. Even when my brother invited him to our shack for the weekend shortly after, I kept quiet. I wanted to protect him from embarrassment and didn't think for a second he would come. I was wrong. All of a sudden, my sacred holiday house at the tranquil beach was no longer.

Everyone could tell he was anxious from the moment he arrived. Yet his compulsion would not let him stay away. He arrived in the morning and after my mother's caring questions, he made an excuse of illness and left. So nervous he backed into my car as he fled the scene.

Raspberry Vomit

It was only a matter of weeks from then things escalated. I had been at college all morning and returned home mid-afternoon. Now by this stage my action about this situation had still been no action. I'd employed the highly ineffective strategy of denial and avoidance.

I unlocked the door with the key I hadn't even moved from its hiding spot in the rock. I had just enough time to register it was unusually dark inside. Mum never drew the curtains through the day. I must have turned to pull closed the door at the instant the log cracked across the back of my skull. I always believed if I was ever in physical danger I would fight but I didn't. I crashed to the ground and things got even darker. I had no idea what was going on and hid my head in impulsive protection. When I opened my eyes, I saw a figure speed off across the front garden all dressed in black wearing a full balaclava.

It felt like hours before my legs would push me up. The phone was plugged into the wall on the other side of the lounge room and I just needed to reach it. My father bear would be at the other end if I could just get there. What I wasn't expecting was that my voice wouldn't be there with me. The first time I tried to call nothing at all came out. Dad muttered something, annoyed he hung up in my ear.

The second time I called I croaked and a squeaky sound fell out. I must have sounded like a nutter, so he hung up again. Somehow with the third attempt I said "Dad". He snapped to attention. We had a brief interaction and I have no recollection of what I communicated but he seemed to understand that I was at home. He instructed me to go down to the backyard and find the builders who were there during the subdivision and wait for him. I still can't recall a single one of their faces but do remember being embarrassed to interrupt them.

Mum arrived home, followed by my brother, followed by the police. One of Dad's fishing buddies was married to a detective from the Criminal Investigation Branch. I was relieved when she arrived with her familiar face. They told me how good I was providing a full description of what he was wearing. The log of wood was dropped on the carpet. The presence of a weapon left so carelessly gave me confidence I didn't imagine it as it had seemed so surreal.

They went on with their questions and what else I told them who knows. I don't know how I explained the door wasn't forced open and I lied when they asked if I knew who had a reason to hurt me. We returned from the police station where I'd done the formal statement and had the photos taken of the non-visible splitting pain in my head. Sitting on the couch not having a clue what to do with myself I suddenly felt overwhelming shame. I felt guilty about the skirt I had worn that day. I knew it was too short. Why did I think it was cute? Why was my tee shirt so short? I have a clear picture of my flowing fabric skirt pattern with brown and black flowers.

Two days passed before I finally admitted I knew it was him. The detectives searched his house and found the clothes I described in the back of his dad's cupboard. He admitted to it after the evidence was recovered. This was not before an initial denial and the lies from his friend who provided him an alibi. I had to go to court for the judge to issue the apprehended violence order. I got so confused even after my lawyer instructed me not to stand in the box for the accused, I went straight up into it. The judge embarrassingly asked if I was the victim or the accused. The judge then asked if I felt in fear and in danger. My performance must have been satisfactory because he issued the order. It felt so contrived and formal, like I was on trial to prove myself, to express my pain and prove I was deserving of protection from the state. I didn't mean to cause any fuss or draw attention.

I didn't return to school for a few weeks. He had dropped out and never made any attempt to contact me. While I was away, an assembly was held and the students informed factually of what had transpired. Mutual friends of ours came to the house. Initially I was happy they would go out of their way to check on me and see how I was. Once I had defended my side of the story for the umpteenth time I declined anymore visits. The last girl telling me he couldn't have meant it and I should forgive the poor guy. None of our male friends came. One guy came up to me in the street to inform me I deserved what I got. Many of my friends just never mentioned it.

This was the first time I saw a professional from the caring sector. As part of the trial I was given one free counselling session as a victim of sexual violence. At 17, I didn't identify with this label. I was stupid for not being aware of his feelings, I gave away too much of my attention to him and I just needed to keep a lower profile and stay away from people then I'd be fine. My mum attended the counselling session and I had few things to say other than confirming this wouldn't happen again.

He was convicted to 90 hours community service and I never did find out exactly what that was. His lawyer asserted he only intended to shock me into being his friend again. Like there was no chance a planned and premeditated strike on the skull with a log of wood at full force by a grown extremely fit man could inflict brain damage or take my life. I've never said that to anyone or said it that way. I never wanted anyone to worry. I was scared. I did learn a valuable lesson that passion is powerful and destructive. Anyone is capable of absolutely everything, even the nice ones. I learned anything can happen to anyone. Life became very small in a moment.

CHAPTER 7

My Hourly Rate

My dad had arranged work experience at a local accounting firm when I was in highschool. I hadn't enjoyed it much. I had planned to move away to do a law degree in a larger city after highschool. After I was attacked my fear had translated into a strong desire to stay home. I decided to be an accountant instead because I was able to study that at home.

I studied at my local campus. I found an undergraduate job in a rival firm and began my journey into the laugh-a-minute world of financial services. I earned half what I did waitressing at our local casino and there were no more chances of after-show photos perched on the knee of the members of Manpower when Jamie Durie was still in the front line. Still, I was on a career trajectory.

I've mentioned my dedication to the best results at school and I translated the determination into my work. It was so easy to please them. The partner I worked for was a wise, owlish type who spent most of his time campaigning to further his Rotary career in preparation for his retirement. He dangled his exit to all the staff and the ambitious amongst us had hopes of retaining his lucrative clients ranging from fourth generation millionaire farmers to up and coming agri-tourism ventures and retailers.

He was big on community service and when I was called to jury duty at the ripe old age of 20 he insisted I do it. Going into the Supreme Court to join the pool of 150 potential jurors I did not expect my number to come up or the solicitor to select me. Wrong and wrong again.

It was quite a lesson in how fucked up the system is. It was a peek into a part of society I had not encountered before. The first trial was an incest case. The victim was now an adult and so the trial was public, and she was required to face the accused, her father. I have the imagined pictures of her descriptions of the nightly ordeal burnt into my mind. To my horror the whole case was abandoned and the jury dismissed when the young victim made reference to something in her younger years which was inadmissible. It related to a trial she had endured as a minor. The victim, the tiny frail shaking young woman now had to wait and face another jury months if not years down the track. She had to wait to face her attacker, her father again. I wanted to be sick.

The second case was another rape case. The victim – a young woman who had been a few years ahead of me at high school and the accused, a local bouncer I vaguely recognised from the pub. It was described as a chance drunken night when they encountered each other outside their building of apartments and had sex in the bushes the other side of the door of the house he shared with his wife and young son. Despite the recounting of the night and her clear inability to give consent the jury could not face the heartbreak of ruining this young man's life. We could not face the torture of his young wife who sat loyally in the court supporting him. We did have to face denying the survivor her closure, healing or whatever it was she was seeking.

We had a *Law and Order* type shut-in, had our evening meal delivered and took vote after vote. If I could go back there now I still don't know what I'd do differently. The whole thing was an awful decision.

The third and final case was thankfully different. The victim was an insurance company who wasn't having a bar of a bogus claim. Two brothers had hatched a plan to secure the money for a nice new house by burning down their current one. OK, yes, the mum was clearly a victim here as the insurance company smelled a rat and pursued a criminal conviction. Luckily, they pleaded guilty and the jury nightmare was over. We were dismissed to return to our lives. It was interesting to participate in our justice system. I'm ever so glad I didn't become a solicitor based on the experience, I wouldn't have lasted a week.

At the firm the more hours I did, the more clients I pleased, the more billable hours and productivity levels I achieved the higher my charge out rate went. What a fun competition it was. I had learned the rules quickly and knew exactly how to win favour with those in power. A move to a better cubical or a 2 per cent pay rise was highly coveted and I won them over and over again. I didn't have time for friends or much contact with family and my husband had a completely different routine to me. Those people who stared across the cubicle divider or into the glass-walled offices became my tribe. There was the funny one, the cute one, the sweet one, the mumma bear and the hot one (husband #2). There was a string of staff who came then went and a few who I know are still there. We worked together and we played together.

We had a social club, pool parties and Christmas parties. The highlight of the year was attending the local horse races at our prestigious car spot on the lawn. If you weren't vomiting on your tie or your bare feet by 3 p.m. you really hadn't tried hard enough.

We knew each other's family and homes, threw baby showers, going away and coming back parties for one another. We were each other's support network all the while remaining aware of where we stood in the delicate hierarchy.

It was the morning teas I remember the most. The sausage rolls and cream cakes. All the things I would stare at, full of willpower if I was on yet another diet. We celebrated at any chance. I'm sure we had morning tea for my jury service. These people were there for me when I got married the first time. They were there for me when I got divorced the first time. They were there for my university graduation and my 21st birthday.

This closeness did present several problems. I was told by one of the partners some years down the track that I had been hired over the other female candidate based on my looks. I have been the object of plenty of praise and admiration. I wish I could say it was for my sparkling personality. When I retort with just that, men say, "Oh yeah, that too". Some "compliments" stick in my mind. Like the time I was 13, at the cinema with mum, and she nipped out to get popcorn. A lovely older gent leant over to inform me I was "a thoroughbred indeed". Cheers mate.

There was a night when a man from work took his chance to put his hand straight down the back of my jeans in the pub while we were surrounded by our colleagues. I excused him as being drunk, and he phoned my husband the next day to apologise to him. I kid you not.

There was the time when the husband of my friend declared in front of her, if he knew me when he was younger, he would have married me instead. I excused him because he was drunk, and we never spoke of it again.

There was the junior staff member who told everyone repeatedly he was in love with me. His manager, who apparently shared the same admiration, encouraged his affection and kept the joke going. I excused it as playing around.

I was 19 when I joined the firm. I didn't understand what I was supposed to do socially and what I had the right to do. The seven years I spent in service of the dollar set up a lot of my social expectations. Work hard, play hard. Anything is tolerated out of work hours as long as you keep your billable hours up. Affairs and alcoholism were normalised. There were emotional breakdowns and breakups. Sounds just like the rest of life. I had not drunk very often before that time. I had previously been too busy to be drinking away a Saturday night or sleeping in nursing hangovers.

When I finished my formal study a few years in I got the big promotion I had worked for. At this point, I questioned why I wasn't having much fun at home. My first husband was completely boring. The years were not helping his momentum in life, and he didn't fit in with my work crowd. I had thought there would be a reward at the end of this rainbow and the best example I found was booze and a breakup.

My first husband had also been a friend of my brother's. He was 19 and I was 14 when we met. He gave me a Valentine's Day card at the speedway one night, and I was interested enough to go on a date. He picked me up at our house in the small town and brought me into the big smoke in his own car. He shouted me lunch at McDonald's (the same one I later embarrassed myself at). I never dreamt it would last and neither did my parents.

I was always in a hurry to grow up and having a relationship and sex was no different. I don't recall anything much other than asking mum how long sex takes after watching the movie Cocktail, where Tom Cruise keeps his lover up all night. I was either disappointed or relieved to hear her clarify it takes about 15 minutes.

Most of my facts about sex were possibly sourced from *Cleo* and *Cosmo* magazines. Not that I couldn't talk to Mum I just didn't really need to because I already knew it all. Now I didn't win the prize to be the first girl in my class to lose her virginity, but I was second. I never spoke to anybody about my early sex life but the girls at school knew I had an older boyfriend and that was enough.

Not wanting to tarnish my rep with any perceived authority figure I kept the shame of this side of my life to myself. I did not have mature girlfriends to talk to about it, so I kept the tired experiences to myself. The first stuff was fun. Hormones racing, fumbling about and new things being tried out. Now, I see those five years age difference meant a lot for the power dynamic. At the time I didn't see it.

It wasn't long after he started the pages and pages of professing his undying love in poetry and song before he started putting the hard word on me. He showed so much commitment to me it was lovely at first. He would buy gold and ruby jewellery and a constant string of other gifts. He would take me out for meals in posh restaurants where I would pretend to be so grown up. He would buy me tickets to anything I would go to with him. Now I guess you would say it was grooming.

He would often call the office at my high school to talk to me because he couldn't make it through the day without speaking to me. He would drive to the school and sit in the teacher's car park and hope he would see me on the basketball court.

My art teacher was a friend of my dad's, so he was the one sent to talk to me about this guy hanging around. He promised not to tell my parents if I made it stop. It didn't stop. He just got sneakier.

My Hourly Rate

The sneakiness extended to taking me deep into the bush and nicking home when his parents were out to do what teenage boys want to do. There wasn't much romance in this part. It was an expectation in return for the showering of affection and generosity. It went on for years and years. I felt both loved and shameful.

We went on to have a marriage, and he was my rock at times. He did so much to love me. It never occurred to me anything was up with our relationship when I was young. To me, it just felt like the way life goes and I ignored almost every icky feeling as I got busier and busier.

CHAPTER 8

The Diamond in the Snail

Doing something irresistable to reduce psychic distress in psychological terms is a compulsion. It was only after moving through phase after phase of my therapeutic journey that I even associated this word with myself. Life continued down roads mapped out for success and achievement, ticked off like tourist attractions on a big old map. Making the hard slog from place to place only to find it didn't fulfil its promise to be the ride of a lifetime.

I did in fact have a gleefully perfect day spent at Paris Disneyland and though fleeting, it's one of my greatest days in memory and fulfilled its promise. Whether it was or whether I now make it so, it doesn't matter one bit. I keep the magical image of me riding those alabaster horses around and around sporting my Mickey Mouse ears.

Graced with Womanhood

I went to Paris during a five-week trip to Europe with husband #2 when in fact he became fiancé #2. We went to dinner at the Mont Marte and a Tiffany diamond found its way into my garlicky escargot. I cried for hours, and he hushed me, embarrassed it might look like we were fighting in front of thousands of tourists who we would never see again.

We had met working at the firm and when I was turning my focus on locating some fun, he appeared top of the list. His boyish charisma and good looks seemed charming, and I was intrigued. He had plenty of attention from girls and it became a competition for me. As was the same with the first relationship I had no intentions of it going anywhere long term. I wanted a laugh, and some new experiences.

We had far more in common than I'd expected and, as it turns out, opposite temperaments. However, I am apparently the marrying kind. We followed the engagement with the sophisticated wedding at a vineyard, had a son, built a mini-mansion and pushed head-on into demanding careers.

All the while I talked more to my journals than I had ever done to him. Being a mother and a wife and keeping a large new home and running a state-wide charity was a fair bit to balance at once.

When we should have been turning to each other for help we seemed to look elsewhere, and we both felt the strain.

When I recently spoke to him about this book we reflected that neither of us exactly remembered details of why we broke up. We chatted casually about this time in our lives. Our son rode his scooter between us, half listening to our reminiscing. My former husband spoke of my passion for my career and how I appeared to him as either operating as 11 out of 10 or -1. Another description for compulsion perhaps. Despite initiating his demotion in my world, I still tear up every time I think of the "us" that was, even now sitting in this annoyingly public café.

The Diamond in the Snail

At the point when we were beginning to separate, the drinking skyrocketed for me. I did not feel well on the stuff and yet it became a daily relaxation ritual and a weekend escape. When I drink, before I throw up, I have a wonderful few anxiety-free minutes, where I can totally relax, eat, dance and sing, have amazing sex or simply fall asleep without trying. Who wouldn't want those things? I did. I had them for the next 15 years.

Booze washed away my compulsions in a matter of moments. As it drained away from my system it gave the compulsions a jump start each and every day starting around 4 a.m. Every morning I would struggle out of bed and bring out the coffee. Coffee, coffee and more coffee until 3 p.m. then wine, wine and more wine until bed. Unless it was the weekend, then the rules were different. This went on a lot, not all the time, but it was the prevailing scenario.

At the end of my second marriage, my crutch was the bottle. At this stage, my body was still holding out, and so I continued to put it through its paces without too much remorse. There was guilt and shame and self-hatred but not enough to stop. After I left my second husband, I found a spectacular apartment overlooking a glorious park looking down the river in the centre of the city. It was the most perfect retreat I could find for myself perched three storeys up and I could almost afford it.

Next door was a bottle shop. The top of today's bottle would be off before I made it up those three flights of stairs. Every morning I would promise I wouldn't buy anymore. I would upon waking tip out any remnants of the night before down the sink. Sometimes full bottles of wine or half-drunk bottles of spirits. I would empty nasty snacks into the rubbish bin making sure to tip them out of their packets, so I wouldn't be tempted to fish them out later in desperation.

All those seemingly laughable habits are performed regularly by people I know too. Social media depicts it as highly amusing and relatable.

It seemed a perfectly acceptable way to cope with my grief. I hadn't breathed a word to my friends and colleagues about my marriage breakdown until almost six weeks after it happened. Choosing instead to trust myself to process it all in written form.

The drinking continued to elevate in my private abode, no one was there to hide anything from. No one asked where the wine had gone or the money. I used to joke about two drinks, and I was anyones. In truth, this never actually happened but my point was it freed my spirit and I shed my reserve. I did try two experimental relationships during this period. What a train wreck they were. Terrible choices. Dangerous situations and more compulsions to cope.

My anxiety peaked with constant shaking which would start at the smallest of things. I would shiver and tense up for hours on end. A song, a smell, the sound of a text message would alert my system to get ready for attack.

It was pure life and death in those moments. The choices I continued to make took me further and further away from my calm and balance. In favour of processing grief and potential healing, I moved on to my next round of fighting for my life. I was going to turn up the fun dial and enjoy this newfound week on week off custody arrangement. It would help me cope with the blinding pain.

The first glass of wine on every second Friday was poured through wet and salty eyes as my son disappeared for another week. It didn't take long for me to find a posse of people only too keen to keep me company at the pub and go dancing until 3 a.m.

I met husband #3, in a local pub. Yet again he seemed like a good way to have some fun. He knew how to party. Carefree yet with all the worries of the world his complexity intrigued me. It was taxing living these two lives each week being poles apart from Mum and CEO and a jokingly titled 'rockstar lifestyle'.

I had certainly found a partner to have fun with. Turns out I am a gig loving person. I enjoyed the tunes of the old faves and the party starters. I travelled the state and the mainland sometimes for gigs in pubs and festivals. I was usually the first one up dancing and singing every word. I can't finish this chapter without telling you that during this time I had a cameo in a professional film clip. If I could go back to tell my 14-year-old self, I would have been pretty stoked.

CHAPTER 9

No Pharos

Much positivism has been written about the benefits of experiencing an emotional breakdown, also referred to as a severe mental health episode. To me, it feels a bit like people saying it's good luck to be crapped on by a bird. This happened to me once. It has been the closest situation to the attack in my dark living room. I was at a street festival in town. The scream that escaped my mouth, that didn't show up all those years ago must have shocked some folks. It bloody hurt when the bird was over 20 feet in the air then let loose its explosion that landed on the top of my head. It didn't seem very lucky. It was an instant trigger to prior trauma of being hit on the head. Cue the anxiety. It took a few glasses of bubbles throughout the afternoon to keep my smiling socialite face in place for the sake of my friends.

It could also be likened to telling someone it's good luck to have rain on your wedding day. In this regard, I felt lucky I had three for three shining summer days.

My first experience with a major mental health event was when I separated from my first husband. The wall of cladding that held me steady in life no longer had the strength to keep me upright. I ran headfirst at getting busy moving on with little warning for anyone. I'd made my decision and every cell in my body was out the door.

I left one day and arrived at mum's cafe announcing, extremely matter of fact, I was moving home. I gave myself a month to find an apartment and get on with it. Without a house or husband to slave over, I soon spiralled into regular drinking on my own. Adding to my cycle times of excited liberation to misery and despairing hangovers.

I saw a psychologist with some regularity for the first time. She was older and softly spoken but her face felt sad, and her advice to slow down and take a holiday on my own seemed utterly boring. I felt as if she couldn't see who she was dealing with. Her caution at starting a fling so soon after the breakup was useless. I just wanted to do something to pull me through the inconvenient levels of grief and anxiety getting in my way.

I found myself a safe little unit in a gated community five minutes from mum and dad's house. I embarked on a relationship and dabbled with a return to the youth. I had never been one for visiting pubs and dancing until the wee hours. This seemed like the logical thing to be done. I had been prescribed a range of antidepressants, making several changes before the side effects of vomiting and passing out during the day subsided. I took no heed however to reduce my regular and binge drinking. Eventually, it all ended in tears and I couldn't face the world beyond my front door.

No Pharos

Looking back, I think this is when the crying started. I had, of course, had moments of tears before but mostly for other peoples' pain not my own. At funerals still, I'm usually the one silently sobbing despite the fact the deceased might have been a friend of a friend. It's the family who brings me undone. For years, I'd decided the only way to avoid this perceived humiliation is not to attend. We've had too many friends and family die before they saw 50. Even before they saw 30. Both by their own hand or fate's cruel one.

I went into work one day and couldn't see the typed words on my screen as my eyes were sore from crying. My face had been swollen beyond recognition. My boss noticeably gasped when he walked into my office. Afterwards I returned only for a farewell party. I'd already been on months of leave. My ruse was up. Seven years down the drain – what a failure. I was not perfect or unbreakable and my colleagues knowing the truth of my weakness was unbearable. I had now been divorced before 30, no longer a winner, no longer a very good girl.

In getting on I found another job straight away and had a new group of people to impress with my fortitude. First, I needed to schedule a pesky holiday with my two weeks' break in between. I was fascinated with ancient civilizations and captivated by hieroglyphs surviving so many thousands of years. So why not Egypt. I was 20-something and had never ever been past the Gold Coast, what a sterling idea! So, I booked, found my passport, bought my backpack and seven days later I was on a plane to the Middle East.

My reckless abandon started before I even got there; I had an eight-hour stopover in Dubai. I saw no reason to miss the chance to see the United Arab Emirates in the flesh. After passing through customs this six-foot-tall blonde girl headed into the downtown Gold Souk and felt like a free woman. Standing in the hustling of glimmering jewellery I felt so anonymous despite towering over men and women alike. I grew three inches (eight centimetres). My travel agent later scorned me with all the could-have-been from my tiny little adventure. She felt it may have ended in disaster, but I still smile at my priceless pictures from that day and my beautiful gold necklace.

Eagerly stretching my long legs when I finally arrived I rushed through the Cairo airport I tried to hide my terror at the toilet-like décor of the airport. With its floor to ceiling white tiles it was stark and horrid. Hordes of people surrounded me, including the serious men dressed fully in black with machine guns. I was meeting a small tour group the next day and a guide had collected us at the airport to get us safely to the city hotel. This is when I met some other travellers. In all, there were eight of us. A mixed bunch of fellow Aussies, me being from the furthest away. There were three others who were escaping the horror of break-ups, so we quickly formed our gang. It's pretty hard to find alcohol in Egypt, so the first night there, there was little temptation.

I have photos of this trip on my wall. I am looking right now at the magical Felucca ride we took on the Nile. There are some of me standing beside the great pyramids at Giza and the Arabic tourists taking photos of me in front of the Sphinx. They seemed amazed that human girls grew so tall and had sand coloured hair. The temples and towns were as enchanting as I had dreamed. The Bedouin people were fascinating and the camel and donkey rides through the small towns were charming. We visited Tutankhamun's tomb and took an epic train ride where the terror of the toilets left us holding on for hours. The Cairo museum was total madness. The relics spread as far as you can see shoved into every available inch of space. People can even touch some, and they seem to be in a constant state of flux. The vast amounts of it all are staggering.

We drove to the Suez Canal on the border with Jordan. We were part of a convoy of buses travelling at daybreak under armed guards at the back and front of the line of coaches. The sun rising in the morning across the Arabian desert filled me with a wonder I'd never experienced and seemed as far away from my life on the other side of the world as possible.

Sharing such fun and exhilaration brought our small travelling family close together. A week felt like a mini life we shared in the blink of an eye. Our guide was a local man in his late 20s who was well practiced in giving the tourists from down under the best on offer in this foreign land. We visited stores owned by his friends in bazaars and cafes who all clearly provided kickbacks on purchases to supplement his tour guide wages. There are millions of people competing for every last tourist dollar in this openly competitive country. He watched carefully for dangers and I felt comforted by the ease he had with the way of life amidst all this craziness.

Over the week, he and I would have quiet chats together. One evening we went smoking shisha in a Luxor café by the river and drinking sweet peppermint tea beside the ocean in Alexandria. He was a contrast to the locals we had encountered. Softly spoken, well-dressed and bearing a sensitivity not a lot of men I had known seemed to have. I was interested in his life, his upbringing and what he wanted to do next.

On the road back from the very popular El Alamein was a shrine with its tanks and graves of Australian soldiers. Afterwards we took a detour to visit one of his personal friends, a pig farmer with a huge plot of land. His home was a mansion, complete with servants, smoking parlours and a huge pool with a swim-up bar. It was well stocked with free-flowing beer and all the local unfiltered cigarettes we could smoke. We were offered luxurious bathrobes and supplied with whatever we desired. We dined on a feast fit to feed the nearby village. Then came the catch. Turned out this farmer wanted a wife, and he had his heart set on a westerner. It became clear this was a regular occurrence in the tour itinerary, and we were today's fresh meat for the viewing. Two of the girls accepted his invitation to stay the night leaving the group to go on without them.

Within the group, there was a mother with her teenage daughter. During the afternoon she pulled me aside and cautioned me to be wary of the farmer as things are very different over here. While somewhat tipsy and tempted to live like a princess for a couple more hours I thought of my mother and knew she would be right. I chose not to stay with those girls. As the rest of us piled back into the bus she grabbed my arm again as the tour guide jumped behind the wheel. She said even firmer this time don't trust him either.

The next was my last night in Cairo. I was flying home the following morning. We had said our goodbyes and swapped our email addresses (pre-Facebook) and agreed to share photos after we got them printed. My local mate had made his final gestures to each of us and when he got to me, he asked me if I'd like to go with him to a jazz club that evening. I was on the last flight and therefore he knew I was alone. Now looking back I know I didn't think it through. I had weighed the pros and cons but remember I was still in my early 20s. So, what the hell. We met in the hotel reception and then made our way through the streets in the hazy masses.

We arrived at a cute little haunt which was probably the cleanest place I had been to since arriving. He bought the first round of drinks while I found us a table. I loved the music and the drinks kept coming and coming. It hadn't occurred to me he was drinking nowhere near as many. From here the pictures are more static than flowing in my mind but next, we moved outside to meet a few of his friends in the car park. Seemed reasonable.

There were two huge guys and a beguiling young Egyptian woman with the prettiest of features and long thick black hair. I was even more eager to talk to a local young woman living in this country. She told me my companion for the evening was, in fact, working day and night to earn enough money to bribe whoever needed to be bribed to free his girlfriend from her now yearlong stay in prison. Turns out she had been dealing drugs. This was Egypt where there is the death penalty, and they don't look favourably on any type of substance. But isn't he sweet? I thought he was so caring and supportive. That's what I honestly thought. Not, "Fuck, where's my hotel? And how the hell do I get back there? Lock the door as quickly as possible."

No Pharos

Removing the fuzz, I know I sat in the back of someone's car and smoked my very first joint. It could have been anything and it was definitely something. I was asked for money in return and my night started to feel more like a transaction than the laugh with a new group of people I thought I was having. After so much booze I was sporting a pretty good buzz. I have never once blacked out from drinking. I always throw up first. So this happened when we got back to my room.

Apparently, the vomiting hadn't been enough to deter him. He had been so gentlemanly and seen me to my door, then to my toilet, then to my bed. This is where I fell asleep. Momentarily anyway. The next thing that happened is sadly probably exactly what you think happened. Remember I said I always thought I would fight if I was attacked and hadn't? Well now was the same. Partly through shock, partly through exhaustion and partly through the inevitability of how shameful my intoxicated behaviour had been.

I was woken in the morning by the cleaning ladies unwilling to come back later. Even though I didn't know them and they would never know me, it was the loneliest and most mortifying feeling. They found me naked covered in blood and vomit, aching all over inside and out. I wish they had yelled at me. Told me how stupid I was and let me cry. They just pottered around and righted the wrongs of the linen while I showered in silence.

I wanted to feel something, but I didn't, only the soreness and aching. After they left the phone rang. It was him. I had read in my travel guide that it's customary to tip the tour guide at the completion of the journey. This is considered part of their salary. He was phoning to collect. How much exactly was that experience worth to me?

I didn't think of the therapy bills, only how many Egypt dollars I could find. I cracked the door slightly and passed over the notes. I glanced up to flash a polite smile so as not to be rude.

In an attempt to find comfort in anything familiar I could only think to head straight for the KFC across the road. I didn't care if I was eating the local stray cat as they joked. I couldn't eat a thing anyway. Then I went to the airport, checked in, passed through customs and took a seat at the gate lounge. I found some blank sheets on the back of my travel notes and I started to write. I wrote every last detail of the past 24 hours. Minute by minute, at least what I could remember. I wrote what I could remember, and I wrote what I didn't, as if I did. Then I stood over a rubbish bin and shredded the paper into hundreds of pieces. I left it there. Together with my memory of it. So I planned…

I had a few days blocked out to stay in Western Australia with a friend on the way home. I moved the flights up to get back home as fast as I could. No one really asked why although I am sure they would have believed my lies if they had. Within the next month I moved in with my boyfriend who was to be husband #2. Clearly, I wasn't to be trusted on my own. Back to the plan of career, house, marriage and then came baby. I hope at least his girlfriend found her freedom.

CHAPTER 10

Life With or Without You

My compulsions continued to grow as my psyche searched with the ever-increasing need to find comfort. My doing was keeping my mind constantly running. My body was being pushed along with it. I had the writing and reading and the aura flooding influence of music and TV.

Sitting under our pool table with my brother when we could still fit, we listened to Mum's ABBA and Neil Diamond records and Dad's Kenny Rogers and Johnny Cash cassette tapes. We sang loudly and I would dance. Both pretty badly. The mood was light and cheerful, and the heartbroken lyrics seemed comical and just words to fit to the tunes. As I grew, my tastes became my own. Saturday mornings always started with *Rage* the ABC TV show, and keeping up with the week's top pop hits. My first real crush was on Kylie Minogue. She was so bubbly and captivated girls across the country.

A friend on a neighbouring farm shared my school bus, and we would make each other mixtapes in the afternoons deejaying the intros to our favourite songs and adding commentary as a track finished. I would play mine back to myself and laugh at my own jokes taking pride in my stellar compilations each day. When I met my first husband, he was addicted to U2 and bound me up in their journey from angry young Irish schoolboys to basically ruling the world. The drummer Larry was my official second crush. As it turns out, I kissed him once. I stood at the green door of Waverly stadium back when it was still standing. Waiting almost first in line hoping to catch a glimpse of the rock stars being whisked away after the show. Much to my utter delight, he himself walked out the door and signed autographs for the adoring fans.

I'd slept out all night in the mall to buy those concert tickets. Not really sleeping at all on the cold concrete ground. I ran up the escalators to the Ticketmaster counter on the fifth floor and I made it there first. I scored seats in row seven and thought I was made. At the concert, I looked at the people in the front row with hatred and when I heard the first note of the first song I just ran. Straight to the stage. As I sang every word and obviously pissed off all the short people behind me, my eyes met Larry's across the stage and I just knew we connected.

So, when he reached me in the line of fans after the show, I felt brave enough to whack a big one on him. Despite his slight shock at my brazen manoeuvre I'm sure he gets it all the time. He was so much shorter than I'd imagine and his nose really quite big but so was my love, it didn't matter. I saw him again only once. In an airport after travelling from Dublin to Nice. I stood frozen when I recognised him. Incognito, he was surrounded by his family. I'm pleased that to say after 30 minutes of staring and debating with my 17-year-old self, I did the respectful thing and left them in peace. Besides, security in airports might not have taken kindly to an unwanted attack of affection.

I listened to Bono and the boys around the clock. I had rare LPs and bootlegs. I had a photo of Larry on my desk in a frame at work. A client once asked if it was my boyfriend. Smiling and embarrassed I wished inside it was true. At that point, I hadn't known I would manifest a drummer love who sings covers of theirs. I was putty in his hands.

My love for U2 looked a little like an obsession I suppose. My experience as a fangirl was so intense I couldn't forgive them when they didn't tour Down Under because they said it was because it was too expensive despite being four of the richest musicians on earth. The next six months I protested in silence refusing to play a single song. I wouldn't trade my passion for anything though. I may not have deeply loved my first husband, but I sure did love those songs.

When I left my first marriage, I walked out without such a big part of my life. That afternoon I left my precious record collection on the lounge room floor. Perhaps without a precious part of myself too. For 15 years I couldn't stand to hear their music. I tried to reclaim it on occasions, but the sadness was epic.

I had cried for the loss of a lifestyle and the memories of happy times, but I never really missed my ex-husband as much as I imagined I would. The loss of those poetic and brilliant songs, however, was rough. Despite my little thing for Larry, we had created a common passion when we hadn't known how to create one of our own. We were kids playing grownups, doing what the grownups did. The songs remind me still of that girl so strong in her love of a source of wonder that was so safely one-sided and only two-dimensional.

My second marriage lasted the longest but the whole relationship ran a similar time frame as the first. We had some super fun times. We both loved being active and outdoors. We would make time to walk our two labradors after our busy days in the office. Both extremely dedicated to our careers we would give each other the space we needed to put in the hours to get our jobs done well. I had put my situational depression behind me and got back on the path our friends were also following.

My depression had been replaced by increasing anxiety but nothing I couldn't disguise. I had plenty to prove in my new job at the charity, and they had plenty of need for me to do it. At first, we were a team of two in the head office surrounded by well-meaning sparsely trained volunteers.

Over the next 11 years, I moved from the accountant to being the first state CEO and the youngest CEO in the country. I had many people directly reporting to me, hundreds of staff and volunteers down the lines and responsibility for everything and, in practice, to everyone.

The first day at work I received two separate interesting phone calls from new colleagues based out of my area. Feeling excited and optimistic I chatted happily without divulging too much. Both were older gentlemen dedicated to their work for this mighty cause-driven organisation. As time moved on, I became accustomed to the ways of the world where volunteers rule and staff can be sometimes treated as a commodity.

Reminding myself off the mission and greater good kept my faith in the work being done. My door was a revolving one and the phone was always ringing. There was always so much more to be done. Every other state and territory had had a CEO for many years already. So, to be offered the role was actually more a formality because I was doing so much of it already.

When the appointment was announced the waves started coming bigger and higher. Those two lovely gents who were so eager to help me from day one ramped up the war they'd decided to wage. To be clear the overall demographic within the situation I'm describing is dominated by retired religious men who had not worked in the not for profit sector or with finance or governance most of the time. I had my favorites of course and my champions for sure but nothing ever came easily. Being geographically widespread made things seem impossible at times. The either passive aggressive or outright aggressive characters worked tirelessly to fight their perceived enemy. I give them credit for their passion and convictions. They had found a sense of purpose and with an uncompromising sense of ownership.

We got up to a fair bit of shenanigans at work. One of the best times was a trip to join the Vietnamese community in Melbourne. There had been a devastating bushfire in our state and our organisation was responsible for elements of the disaster recovery. It had been a difficult time for staff and volunteers, emotionally impacted as they gave so much of themselves to the effort. I had colleagues from other states who reached out to me, but we were making a lot up as we went. There was a mountain of monetary support and donations of goods rolling in. We filled entire warehouses with goods, and all of these needed to be sorted and much of it taken to landfill. All of this needed to be managed. Government relations, negotiations, and the media were constantly taking my attention. It was one of those times people kept going and collapsed once it was finally over.

The Vietnamese community held a fundraiser of their own and donated several thousand dollars to our appeal. In return, they asked me to go to an event in our honour, and they would have further funds raised to hand over. So off I set with my colleague to Melbourne, and we dressed up in our finest. Travelling in the taxi the two of us grew increasingly worried as we drove through the underwhelming suburbs thinking we may be facing disappointment after the excitement had built up.

We arrived at a building which was very plain from the street and something from a Hollywood movie of *Cleopatra* through the doors. With grand pillars and floor to ceiling fine decorations it was a sight to behold. There were black ties and women ready for the Oscars everywhere. We were placed at the head table and supplied with wine. We drank and laughed and were treated as distinguished guests. Less glamorous was when my friend next to me almost died embarrassingly choking on one of the spicy dishes. Then there was the moment we realised in our joyful state we were the only ones boozing along. Apparently, they honour the Chinese New Year and refrain from alcohol for the week. Whoops it was too late by then.

Next, I was summoned to the stage and addressed the ginormous crowd with the story of the suffering and trauma while gazing at the opulence in front of me. After speaking, I was asked to be interviewed on the Vietnamese television station I had no idea existed. Goodness knows what I said.

Once the nerve wracking formalities were done, the music got going and so did the ladies. Imagine for a moment, a room, well a ballroom, of Vietnamese women dressed in jewelled gowns line-dancing, with cowboy hats. Of course, they dragged the two of us in the middle of it all. As two six-foot-tall girls with no talent for line dancing the video is pretty special.

The team gave more of themselves to the organisation than I had seen anywhere in the corporate world. Our families, our lives became embroiled in the values and missions we perhaps aspired to, rather than achieved. It was my experience having a role bestowed on you brings with it all the perceptions surrounding the ideal. Both from yourself and others around you. What it meant to be a CEO had a different meaning to different people. One common instance was if someone approved of an action, they claimed it was their doing. If something went wrong, it was all my responsibility. I believed it too. You can imagine this young first time, female, first ever CEO drowning in the responsibility. If I didn't know how to fix something, I would learn. If I hadn't been aware of something, I would find out. If I didn't have time to get something done, I would take it home and make time.

When I had my son, I took a few months leave. We had lovingly anticipated his arrival and I relished this time we had together. I look back at the memories with my mother's anxiety going through the roof but also with a peaceful, contained focus and purpose. Arriving back into my job with a baby at home required an even bigger juggling act.

I felt my way of being sliding further into very separate pieces. I was pretending to be in control, perfect and ultra-professional at work. Truly, my love of making cookies and playing in the sandpit was really what gave me my purpose. I felt trapped. I knew for 100 per cent certainty I had made it in an amazing career. I had a highly coveted role in a male dominated space in community service and social justice, all the while making it look easy.

The response people gave me when they found out what I did was seductive. I practiced humility as I did not feel I had any right to be boastful, this just seemed to swell their awe. I pushed issues no one else had dared to, and I did whatever I could to impress and befriend those who could make it all happen. The organisation feeds the vulnerable and houses the homeless among hundreds of benevolent acts. It was hard not to love the drive when this was the prize.

However, it was a prize never won because there will always be people who are hungry and people who are homeless despite the austere commitments from people in power.

Over the years we took the cause to the masses with state-wide TV campaigns, media press conferences and lobbying Canberra. I had two separate private lunches with then Prime Minister Tony Abbott. He's much taller than I expected. At both small round table events I was the only woman other than his Chief of Staff. He singled me out in front of the men both times and congratulated me on being in the room. The Chief of Staff sat next to me and, being a fellow tall gal, was compelled to encourage me to ask Tony for what I came for.

We won grants, grew in favour and built an army of outstanding staff who felt empowered to do their jobs. I had figured out this game too. I could plan and strategise the shit out of anything and if I could, put in the hours. All the while I had board reports and staff appraisals, funding contracts and acquittals, financial statements, governance policies, safety audits and procedural checklist to write or review and oversee, to name but a few.

With people coming from every direction all day long, when did I get all this done? Before and after work. One morning I was running rings in my office when an impolite volunteer called to let me know he'd been canvassing his buddies, and he thought I should hear from him that, "Everyone liked me, it's just you aren't very good at your job." He wasn't one of the pair from the first day but was now part of their gang. I politely thanked him for his concern and then cried behind my locked door. Another man rang on my very last morning, before I was taken out for lunch as a parting thank you. Between spitting out a goodbye he insisted, "It is a disgrace to waste money on staff lunches." Between my tears I thought of all the Christmas parties he had attended over the years.

I had a staff member scream at me one day in front of the whole office for "being the worst boss ever". I hadn't made enough time to hear her concerns. I terminated the employment of dozens of staff and was faced with their wrath. I've had people spread untrue gossip and say one thing to my face and do the opposite as soon as they leave. Nothing was ever quite as was decreed on the values' statement hanging in our office.

In the corporate world I understood the aim was to make money. Make money for the client and they were happy. Make money for the bosses and they were even happier. So, this was insane. We all saw the need. We all heard the crippling stories and wanted to help. Yet the actions and way of being of these people was unfathomable to me. For year upon year I smiled and wrote perfect newsletter articles or appreciative emails praising their achievements and success.

After a few years in the role, I realised it was true that the body keeps score and mine had struck out. My drinking was persistent. I had turned away from my husband. I felt distant from my son. I would sit in my office and shake. Do you know how much energy it takes to quiver all day? I had returned to old habits of restricting food and over exercising and shredding my fingers daily. I would look down and see blood and feel shame and embarrassment not noticing what I was doing. Handing board papers to my chairman covered in blood. Your hands are phenomenal. I could pick the skin from around my nails and bite it all the way throughout the day and overnight it would heal. I would drop blood on documents or on my shirt and you know no one ever said a thing to me about it. I went through packets and packets of band-aids.

I had manicures and false nails in the hope it might stop but as soon as they grew out it started again. I would do it in my sleep and occasionally catch myself doing it through sex. I tried hypnotherapy. I was basically walking through a guided meditation to relieve anxiety. In response to the therapists prompts I visualised a purple blob with a face and asked the monster to leave. We wandered onto food and my mum's famous elephant cake. Using food was a method of control I employed since I was a young girl, it was relevant to my anxiety. Sadly, this experience didn't do much for my poor fingers or my love of the elephant cake I would not let myself eat anymore.

When I walk through the city, I often end up taking a route by a special Victorian mansion in the middle of town. Halfway through my time in the role my work buddy hatched a plan. It is now operated as a home away from home for patients and hospital visitors who've travelled from out of the city. I wrote successful pleading proposals to raise the investment capital and pitched the whole thing to the powers that be. We purchased the homestead from a corporation in Singapore and I'd say it was my largest international transaction to date.

On our first visit to the mansion we were struck by the old worldly charms maintained in its 150-year-old style, including intricate plastering, chandeliers, brass wall plating, stained glass windows, floral carpet, ornate staircases and then there was the ivy. The whole double storey eastern side was covered in the menace. Lulled by the romantic wonders walking into an upstairs bathroom we were greeted with the vines stretched like hands of zombies growing through the vents ready to grab us. I think we both screamed and then probably laughed.

On one of those early days my colleague saved my life. We had been about to leave when she yanked me at her full force back from the side porch as I took one step out the door. As it slammed behind us the windowpane in the centre of it filled with bees as they swarmed down the driveway. She's a damn legend with lightning reflexes, that one.

We scrubbed that place with all our might as it became our pet projects. We engaged contractors and anyone who would volunteer to help. When my trusted electrician gave me the quote for the rewiring, I felt my imaginary ulcer scream at me. It was an anxiety response, but I was convinced my guts were exploding. I researched a little and realised ulcers were actually caused by bacteria so miraculously the pain eased.

I believed with enough moments of humor and joy and enough hours of sleep I would be okay. I had my strategies to keep healthy, but I was swinging between ignoring and obsessively enforcing them. Whenever I claim to be close to ticking the box on my life's 'to-do list' at work or at home I would be soon rushing straight at the next one.

The more you drink the more you need to drink to get drunk. The more restrictions you make of your food the more restrictions you must make to be skinny. The more sex you have the more thrilling it needs to be to get turned on. The more clothes you buy the newer the clothes you want to look just perfect. All the victories felt meaningless. They kept me very busy and not one eased pain for more than a few hours at best.

CHAPTER 11

The Good Stuff

On the night I met husband #3 I had been on the couch hungover and exhausted deciding what excuse I could use not to go out as I promised. I called myself some unkind names and dragged myself off feeling better with some makeup and my new high heel boots. I felt sure some hair of the dog would do the trick. We first ate a sensible meal before leaving the friends who had to go home to their children. We had dancing to locate.

After catching my married friend in the toilet sending boob pics to a fly in, fly out NBN installer, I was beginning to question if the whole world of dating was just too ridiculous.

On that morning I'd returned from visiting an on again-off again, kinda-sorta boyfriend. A friend of a friend of someone I knew. We had been introduced a few years before and after divorce number two he looked interesting. A new source of fun, he was absolutely totally not going to be the sort of guy I would form an attachment to. He was the type of sailor who had a girl in every port and he travelled a lot. Don't ask what the appeal was. Perhaps it was a social experiment in my own behaviour to see if I could have a relationship casually. Maybe he was just so damn sexy I didn't want to resist.

I thought it would be great with no strings to worry about, and just have some fun. Alas, it was not so easy. Between his kids, his divorce, his work, his mental health, he had so much to share and I was a cheap therapist. He was really suffering, and I think he was using me to ease the pain and I let him do it. The need to be needed was strong with this one. I would answer his calls day and night. I mistook it for intimacy and closeness grown from the bedroom. When he told me he loved me and I was "different from all the others", I bought it.

It was a skeptical purchase but I wanted to believe. I went from "hell no" to "maybe this could work?". One morning he left his phone on the bench charging while taking a shower, a very unusual event. When I saw the notifications from his dating apps appear one after the other, my heart sank. I wanted to leave with my dignity intact; not having given him any satisfaction of providing a lame-ass explanation. The rage swelled and I couldn't keep quiet. To his credit, he didn't deny it confessing with a hung dog face.

It would feel better to say I never saw him again but it would be a lie. I was seeing a psychologist at the time and she sent me home with a book to read straight away. I had told her this guy was seeking help. He was struggling to adjust, and he needed me. If not me then who else? The co-dependency had developed pretty quickly between him and I given the circumstances. When I read the book with all its warnings and alarm bells for girls with high empathy, I heard all the ways I could help him and none of the ways I could help myself.

The Good Stuff

The last time I saw him was on that weekend I'd gone to him for a hot rendezvous. We had partied all night and slept all day and I'd done everything he'd asked of me. Let me tell you, he asked quite a lot. When I left for my flight, I knew I had to get it together. I was broken and hungover like never before.

In the end I had a laugh with the girls dancing in the pub. As the band packed up I walked home to my apartment, perched in the park trees, ready to leave men alone forever more.

I slept the entire next day. Then the entire week. My chest had given in and I sounded like a rabid bear with a bone lodged in his throat. I took it as a sign, intended or not, to be kinder to myself. I set my sights back on my work and as far away from a love life as possible.

There was no shortage of work to be done and a shortage of people to do it. As I felt more and more out of my depth, I took on additional study to build legitimacy with myself and everyone else. Without a relationship to eat into my precious hours I could be so much more productive. Productive and lonely. I refused to feel any pain and it had still not caught up with me. I'd managed to outsmart it and kept running away. A couple of months in and I thought what the hell, I'll look up the guy from the pub. Surely it would be a bit of fun. I was blind to the pattern, or at least chose to be.

On our second date he asked me while walking in the park if I would go with him on holiday with six of his friends. They had bought a holiday package to a Pacific Island at a charity auction and were leaving in four weeks. Here it was, the fun I had been waiting for. I had been offered the joy of adventure and hilarity with the bonus of helping this depressive boy forget his troubles with an utterance of one word: "Sure!"

What a merry band we were from the trip onwards. We swam, and we sang, and we laughed, and we danced. We drank kava, and we drank everything we had and then everything else we could find. We had a perfect villa on the ocean complete with a reef. The time was spent snorkeling and surfing, and riding on the back of the ute that came with the villa. We forgot what the world was up to and the people back home.

With this new posse there were gigs and parties and weekends away. I became fast friends with his friends, and I'd forgotten what it was like not to dance every weekend. I really did love it. I loved all the happiness, all the hugs, all the dancing. The people who came out to let down their hair and take a break from their day jobs, their worries and just drink. Always drinking.

We settled into a double life. One week I would be a doting mum enjoying the beautiful forest across the road with my son; riding bikes everyday, playing on the park equipment and walking our dog. It was a gorgeous time in his childhood for me. He wanted my full attention, we would paint and make costumes from boxes and play Uno and Monopoly for hours. He was oblivious to my stress, he was my escape from it. I joined him at a playful younger age and felt such freedom and joy to have him with me.

I would pine for his company and cry for the entire first day when he returned to his father. I would use the other week as adult time to enjoy grown up fun and party more and more. This double existence was exhausting. I would have such starkly different roles to fill and would have trouble adjusting each time.

I would spend a lot of nights alone during this period while my musician was out doing his thing. Night after night home alone on the couch. Alone with my wine, chips and *Battlestar Galactica* or *Breaking Bad*. Drinking to pass out, I would often miss the last half of an episode. Then I would go to bed, but I could never sleep properly no matter the amount I had drunk. I would stir and wake hourly. This continued for five years and my body became gravely exhausted from the anxiety and grieving for the half a mother I didn't get to be.

The Good Stuff

Three months after I'd moved in with husband-#3-to-be there was a death in his family. This new family of mine was broken and mourning, and I was there to be part of it all. No one ever asked me how it affected me. Why would they? Their pain was so raw.

The week of the death, my partner's extended family arrived from across the world and spent this time in our standing room only dining area to which I was also a stranger. They barely noticed I was there.

Work had been beyond bearable and I had been headhunted to run another not for profit organisation. Seduced by the sales pitch from a well-established mentor of mine, I was convinced I could do the job. Another big CEO role I was neither prepared nor qualified for. Still, I was desperate to jump ship and the more challenge the better. Being courted for a job is always wonderful and my interest was piqued. During my courtship the organisation was sold to an interstate buyer and I would no longer be my own boss or work for a local organisation. However, I stepped over my doubts and accepted the role at the insistence of my mentor to "give it a go".

I named my price and signed the contract. Then came the death. My will evaporated that morning my partner called me at work to tell me. What was I doing? What was the point? My burning desire to succeed left me right there. I walked out the door.

The next morning, I rang my new boss to be and told him I'd had a change of heart. He was gentle and understanding and only asked me to call him when I was ready to reconsider. He was sure I would. I went to my current boss and told him I was leaving anyway. It was clear to them all I was not in a good way. They were understanding. I know deep down they didn't want to make it harder for me.

I went home that afternoon and quietly confessed what I had done. It was a complete shock, but my partner hardly reacted. No one seemed to notice the condition I was in amongst the gang of strangers gathered around my kitchen table. To me this was the perfect anonymous maneuver.

Adjusting to being home all day was a challenge. My will to perform and be successful was in the past. Most days I didn't recognise the woman I was confronted with in the mirror. The white skin, the acne, the thick black rings under my eyes seemed like another person.

Upon leaving, I was fairly compensated for my troubles at work. I had never made a fuss in all those years I'd been there. It was for the best, I thought at the time, and now. For the greater good of the organisation and the people we served. Perhaps not for the greater good of all the staff around me and those to come.

At that point I wanted to lie down and never get up. I felt lost and I had no faith I could help myself find a way out of it. So began my journey into more and more therapy. I was going to find a way to heal my body and my soul of all this misery. My doctor referred me to a psychiatrist for assessment because the antidepressants she prescribed weren't doing the trick. This is when I started collecting health professionals. My experience remains when you have a field of expertise you see it in the presenting patients. Many of them had answers for me. I didn't know who to trust and the contradictions were often profoundly so.

I gave over my power to my husband at times and I wanted him to be right. I hated seeing my friends without my work to share with them. I felt like an utter worthless failure. From such heights I had fallen.

The money was running out. At rates of up to $500 an hour this entourage of caregivers was bleeding me dry. The organic veggies, legumes, colloidal minerals and prebiotic tonics weren't helping my budget.

The Good Stuff

I tried to straddle both philosophies of healthcare and it occupied most of my time. Rushing from meditation to reflexology and then off to my psychiatrist was a full-time job.

While some medications were harsh I had amazing success with the mood stabiliser early on. I didn't know it was possible to sit still without an ever-present agitation compelling me to move. The closest time I've experienced this level of calm was the magical two drink window before the third drink draws me back to the familiar agitation.

I hid this ever-increasing cocktail of medication from everyone. I could not bring myself to admit I was taking mood stabilisers, antidepressants, antipsychotics, anti-anxiety and sleeping tablets. I don't think in truth I could admit it to myself. I would sound like a crackpot for sure. It wasn't helpful I was drinking either and I didn't want anyone to suggest I stop. I knew it would usually be disastrous, but I didn't want to feel different to everyone else. Alcohol, of course, is prolific in the world for a reason and I had not yet extracted myself from the claws of addiction.

From here, nothing seemed to go well. It felt like I'd screwed up every part of my life. I had to share my son who was the light of my life. I'd thrown away my greatest love in his father. I'd ended my career. I'd abandoned the house I built. With all of it I'd lost my identity. I was thin at least but I was too tired to get to the beach in my tiny bikini. I had an underlying resentment, but I wouldn't give in on another relationship. I was in no position to go through another breakup. That was not an option. A relationship that seemed so liberated in the beginning was pretty impractical to live with.

Our friends were caught by surprise when I eventually left. Why wouldn't they be. No one knew what he was like with me privately and no one knew me well enough to really have a clue. I'd reinvented a new me in this new world. My family, on the other hand, had been waiting it out. They were ready with the spare rooms for the third time taking in my son and me yet again.

I remember all the stress I imagined about leaving, the packing, the judgement, the cost and the unbearable loneliness. In the end it was just a relief. I guess practise makes perfect. Don't misunderstand, it was brutal and devastating and so much hard work. Now I could face myself in the mirror again.

I'd seen a counsellor for four years and in my time with her, nine out of ten times we would talk about my relationship. My psychiatrist knew I needed to stop drinking before I could get back on track and tackle my marriage problems powerfully. I tried to quit alcohol, but it was so ingrained in my life and, honestly, it was the one true escape I had. I had failed in every attempt to give it up.

Eventually I agreed to a week in the clinic to try a new drug and step out of my life to see how it felt. My doctor visited me every night in the hospital and while surrounded by every form of mental illness in the group therapy sessions, I felt like a fraud but also quite at home and actually safe. My doctor had told me how strong I was and reminded me of my creativity, my intelligence and my devotions as a mother. I didn't believe any of this at first. As the week went on, I wondered just ever so slightly if I could actually do something to alter my current plan, I'd been so sure I couldn't let go of.

CHAPTER 12

I'm Not About Waiting

When the primary school assistant principal told me my son was in a fight I did not agree with her perspective on the events. He stood up for himself, and I was so proud. She said he went from 1 to 10 and over reacted. He told me he could've hurt them a lot more. I believed him. I think he was measured in his reaction. I don't blame him at all for then trying to leave the school and walk home after the fight. I would've done the same thing.

It seems to me children and animals occupy a different universe. I've had a life filled with them. We had countless dogs who came and went from our home as a child. Often, they left us to move to a farm, even though we had a farm. Among them a German shorthaired pointer, a springer spaniel, and a golden labrador all found along the way. There was an aloof British blue cat named Perkins who made royal appearances when he felt in the mood. There were budgies who occasionally looked different when my brother and I got home from school. The mesmerising goldfish I've housed were too numerous to recall.

As I sit here, my lap is filled with a kitten and my keyboard is trampled by his mother. Two fluffy cats with their long white coats and mauve blue glimmering eyes. When I hold them my stomach and the tension in my neck loosens. My heart swells just a bit. I couldn't get through an entire book without a nod to them.

My dog succumbed to old age a couple of months ago. 14 years ago, there was a day I decided our five-year-old dog needed a friend. I opened the paper to see an advert for a puppy and there she appeared. A young black labrador up for grabs. Husband #2 was not convinced. I jumped in the car alone and went to see anyway. I pulled up outside the house. He pulled his car into the curb behind me. When we saw her, we knew we could not leave her in her current conditions, so I bundled her into my car. At 14 years old, she'd outstayed any man in my life. The gentlest soul I've ever known, with big brown eyes and a snuggle for everyone. The walks and swims we took were just the best. The day she went I shared this story with my son and thanked my former husband for the second-best gift in life he had shared with me.

My son holds our kitten when he is upset. With his adoring kitten face he licks him on the chin and settles him quickly. They're well worth the scratches on the couch and the hair on my jumper. They are our therapy cats. Their unashamed demands for affection remind me to ask for what I need. Even when I fear I am bothering someone.

I have returned to my childhood through being a mum and create new memories for my inner child. Reading aloud picture books, building Lego fighter jets and drawing cartoons with fat pencils. Being called into the ocean when it's too cold to dare. Hanging at skateparks

I'm Not About Waiting

and the gaming shops. Playing *Pokémon* for hours on end. Learning all their names like Jigglypuff, Meowth and Snorlax and bagging a rare Pikachu. Riding my bike on muddy pump tracks and going to aquariums and zoos.

Kids are the best reminders of how to be free, you don't need to have one to see it. In the beginning I had looked at my son's childhood as an education for which I am responsible. It's my job to protect, teach and show him how to be around people and what he should do. When we did the activities I planned for him, I used them as lessons. There is a skill to be learned and a value to obtain.

It is he who's shown me how to be free. He wants what he wants. He wants to do what he wants to do. He is interested in some things and just not in others. He doesn't do anything for longer than he wants to and rests when he needs to.

He used his birthday money to order scooter bars online. I queried the extra $15 he paid for the express post? "I'm not about waiting," he declared.

He eats when he's hungry, whenever that is. He devours tomatoes like apples and says no to ice cream often. He'll sit down when we're walking when his legs get too tired. He'll laugh when others don't and not when he's supposed to. If he doesn't like the smell of a house or the mess in someone's living room, he'll say so and walk out.

Sometimes he gets lonely, an only child. He wants to be included and inclusive. He will not put up with unfairness, and he enforces his rights as he sees them. He has a temper and he cries. He will fight if provoked. He'll run away if he's triggered and cause adults to worry but doesn't let that stop him. We snuggle almost every night on the couch. I still cry every second Friday morning and make any excuse I can to see him on the week he's with his dad.

Graced with Womanhood

He gets up as soon as he wakes up and cuddles his cat until he's as hairy as him. He has one favourite hoodie he wears every day. He scores off the charts for maths but doesn't like story writing so doesn't try much at that.

He learned the euphonium by playing one hour a week. He wouldn't practice and didn't care; he was pretty good considering his lack of time invested. He was building and programming robots years before his peers. He won't make the bed. He has a YouTube channel for his 3D printing and Fortnight wins. He commentates his video clips but won't speak loudly enough in a cafe to order a drink.

I left his father when he was two. He says he doesn't remember. I asked him recently what his first memory is. He told me he can't tell what's a memory, or a picture he's been shown. His entire childhood is on file in jpeg and iMovie. Have I cheated him from these memories or provided him with more than he may naturally have had?

When I had trouble conceiving, I started researching of course. Turns out a few drinks at the races was all I needed. When I was pregnant, I had websites and books to read and classes to do. He came a week early after two days of initial stage contractions. He was facing upwards and we had an emergency caesarean.

I couldn't brestfeed despite all I'd learnt. There wasn't a cure for the shock of the birth and post-natal anxiety anywhere I could find. I had eight nights in the private hospital suite. We were the only inhabitants for the week and had around the clock care from the midwives. I left the hospital weighing considerably more and without any milk.

At home, I would not give up. Preferring to feed with a tube taped to my boobs and express on a non-stop loop for six weeks. He would sleep on my tummy, and then we'd try again. My weight was distressing me, I needed to fix it. I couldn't fix the feeding, but I could fix myself. I walked up and down the steep hills of our neighbourhood. Pushing the pram with the stitches still in. I would walk until lightheaded and aching. It worked to move the weight.

I cleaned every day, unable to sit with dust on the bookcase or washing in the basket. Much is spoken about postnatal depression. Surprisingly little about postnatal anxiety. Having had anxiety as my companion all my life, it was unlikely to disappear now. Now I had the house, my body and the baby to keep perfect. Fatigue and worry are expected of new parents. It felt like I had no right to feel any other way. As if it were the undeniable reality of the situation. There was no reprieve.

I went to a work Christmas party as my first social outing since giving birth. Man, I did not want to go. My first drink since the lucky night. I survived, of course. Now the lid was off the bottle again.

I returned to work when he was eight months old. The maternity leave pay was up. I took him for the first time to the day care centre the week before. Off we went with tears and apprehension. Well, did I, I mean. We sat down on the mat and looked at the toys. Within the first five minutes another child walked up to us and smacked my son across the face with a metal xylophone.

In a café I cried to my husband and pleaded, "I can't leave him. I don't need to work."

However, that's what I said I would do. We had plans for a new house. There was also my career. There seemed no room to change now. Everything had changed for me though. My mum had assumed I would give up my job once my baby was born. I was angered at her statement. All those years of study. All the hours at work. She'd known. She was right. The moment he came into my life the whole game shifted.

Back I went as per the plan. I didn't practice much self-care. I didn't really know how. My husband was wonderful. We shared the load. They would have one on one time, so I could go to the gym. My time for me. Time for my fat arse and jiggly tummy. I had gained 20 kilograms during pregnancy (and in the hospital). After a lifetime of dieting I had given myself permission to do what my body asked for. The nausea and tiredness were slightly appeased with food. It felt great just to eat.

There was a prenatal diet of course, all the dos and the don'ts. Darrell Lea fudge was on the do for me. By the third trimester room in my stomach quickly ran out. I would still be so hungry. I was allowing myself to eat what I wanted but it wouldn't fit in. Tiny amounts and I'd be stuffed. So, I made it fit in. I realised from this experience compulsions are re-triggered in all kinds of ways.

I had focussed my efforts so strongly on restriction for 15 years. The return to binging and purging seemed harmless this time. I had a reason. It made sense; I was growing a person. Once the baby was born, I'd be right. It would just clear up like a cold sore.

The binge-purge cycle had never fully disappeared from my life. It often happened when drinking. It didn't concern me too much. It was fairly common to be sick on a big night out. The relaxing effect of the alcohol lowered my powers of food restriction. I would eat and eat. Platters and bar snacks destroyed at a frenzied pace. I would hardly taste the salty snack or the sugary treats, but I knew they were good. Then in secret I'd be sick. Problems solved. No calories. No hangover. At least so I hoped.

I functioned this way for the next ten years. It's how I managed to stay out until 3 a.m. on work trips and make the 9 a.m. meetings. It was how later I could stay late at pubs, when drinking I could easily find a buddy or two. Even with only my drink for company I never felt alone.

My son's father and I built a magnificent home. We secured a mortgage ambitious enough to tie us to our careers. It had everything we dreamed of, and we spent hours on the design, picking fittings meticulously, shopping for new appliances and furniture, falling in love with every tap fitting and door handle.

When we moved in, our son was eighteen months old. It was shiny and new. It took hours from my day to keep it that way. Panicked it would lose its perfection. I would be cleaning and polishing, tidying and scrubbing what was already clean. We became a tag team and we didn't see each other much. We did not talk much either.

After I had returned to work I took on a leadership program run over the course of a year, not long after we moved in. A brilliant opportunity I was quite sure I did not deserve. Racked with nerves and highly self-conscious I arrived at day one. A glorious residential setting and 23 more important people than me.

Of all my experiences of synchronicity the most baffling took place in a women's prison as part of this leadership program. We visited various operational sites across the range of sectors. One was the state prison. We saw the male compound and then the females in our group were allowed to visit the women's prison. It was absolutely nothing like I imagined. The male facility was exactly what I'd imagined.

The women were kept in what felt like a group home with barren bedrooms locked from the outside. They had a common room which felt like anyone's lounge room and were sitting together on couches watching the local news. There were six women in total. We walked in and literally just had a moment to be greeted and one of them interrupted saying, "Isn't that you?" Sure enough at that very second, there was my smiling face banging on about a big fundraising and awareness event I had pulled off the previous night. Managing the bushfire recovery was the longest, toughest, most harrowing experience I've had in a work role, and this fundraiser was easily second.

Other states within our organisation had employed teams of people to roll out and host this new fundraising and advocacy campaign.

I had resisted running it for the first two years because we didn't have the resources. Finally, by year three I figured a plan to do it. The plan was pretty much for my closest colleague and I to just do it. We lived and breathed it. We held pre-fundraiser fundraisers, we phoned half the town, we managed the logistics, administration, marketing, PR, media and whatever other stuff there was to be done. The entire team in the organisation were marvelous and supported us in any way they could. It was so much fun and I could talk about the issues all day long.

The topic was banned at home as I compulsively watched the online donation tally rise. The night of the event was magical in a touching and inspirational way. The staff, volunteers, participants, donors, guests and beneficiaries all together for one purpose. The sense of togetherness was actually pretty rare and amazing to have it that night. We pulled the event off four years in a row before I left the organisation. It still runs.

Walking into a room with a group of incarcerated women was more nerve racking than I had anticipated. I worried it would seem disrespectful to be there, like staring at creatures in the zoo.

When those women in the gaol made the connection to me their response was so warm and heartfelt. They acknowledged my work and the contribution the organisation has made to the community. It was an equalising and humbling moment. It's a funny old universe.

The program turned into an experience I adored. I adored the other participants, facilitators and all they were. I expanded my vision and I enlarged the picture of the me I wanted to be. I decided I wasn't a stay at home mum and wife after all.

The group talked and drank, laughed and drank more. I experienced the sort of openness and sharing I'd spent years hiding from. We had our own language, our new memories and our new friendships. This added a new level to my busyness. I held it together so well until it all fell apart.

People ask why I left my second marriage. It's never simple to say. These things rarely are. We separated a couple of times and tried couples' therapy. I was not open to it working. I was walking through the motions I needed to take in order to finish it. The single hardest moment of my life was when I turned away from my sleeping baby and left him.

At the time, I didn't have the language to know how to cope. It was as if my mind had splintered off and I stepped outside of myself. I thought at the time it was really me. My reality was dampened yet I thought I was in control.

These experiences of cognitive disassociation grew in frequency and severity. I would eject myself from situations as if watching TV. The hormones released would flood my system. It felt like being drunk to a degree. It was protective in high stress situations at home and at work. I was careless and carefree. From the outside no one seemed to notice.

When a therapist explained what she saw happening to me, I thought it was bullshit. An excuse for poor behaviour. I was not ready to be excused. I was also not willing to admit the moments of created strength and determination weren't really me either. Not me at my core.

In one of these moments I finally left my husband for what would have been the fourth time and didn't go back. People now marvel at the way we are together as a former couple. We were very different in nature but forgave each other with time just the same. We got on with co-parenting our gorgeous son and laughing together whenever we can.

CHAPTER 13

Miracle #2

In the wake of three divorces I have realised I was going through life relating to my brain as a tool, my will as a weapon and my body as an ornate machine.

I imagined being kinder and more compassionate. First of all to myself. I blamed myself for being stupid and not knowing how to take care of myself. In truth, I did always know, I chose not to listen.

I can point to times where I have been given access to regain my power. I do not have one main thing I credit. I have hundreds of actions, big and little amassed from a study of self-mastery. Such a funny term which has become so vital to me. How obvious it should be we know ourselves best. How obviously we don't.

We forget the first years of our lives as the brain moves on to more important things. These memories instead become part of our body and our being lodged deep in our psyche. To be a functioning adult it is my experience we need to be curious about ourselves at every age to be closer to knowing ourselves now.

Each of us has our stories and none more valid than the other. At the time, for every one of us, these stories can be real and significant. No matter how far I moved past particular times in my life, there's been a recurring sense of loss and a calling I could not speak and had not answered.

Moving into a new relationship after three divorces, I kept that up. Whenever we were together, I had the sweet joy of romance, the laughter of close friendship and the bliss of intimacy. Then I was tested again. Tested to do things I don't like. To be with people I'd rather not. To show interest in topics that don't really faze me.

I have had miserable times on my own at the end of the relationships, hot in the breakup mess, alone and crying. Drinking and eating too much, losing weight, hair and colour. No wonder I didn't want it ever again. I never took the chance to get over the grief on my own. The next potential boyfriend was there, and it was too good a proposition not to explore.

Of all the scenarios I worried about when getting into a new relationship after three divorces, I was hit with a situation that wasn't one of them. The Covid-19 pandemic no one saw coming.

Even when it began to spread through the world, I wasn't concerned it would make its way to me. Not to my shy little island at the bottom of the planet. But then it did.

At this point I still wasn't worried it would impact my family. The numbers were horrible but the chances personally were still way less than dying of a heart attack.

Miracle #2

Then the collective anxiety of society sent my town into madness and also into solidarity, brought together in a frenzy of slowing down and staying at home. What I did not foresee was being isolated indefinitely from the rest of my people including my new lover. Everyone but my son, his dad (Husband #2) and his pregnant new wife.

When I previously lay awake at night fearing heartbreak yet again, I ran through the dangers not wanting to repeat the past and I was thinking of all the relationship disaster stories I had ever heard.

I would brainstorm any and every eventuality then assess the likelihood of the risk occurring and the severity it might have. Throughout the relationship I kept my eye on those ever-present dangers.

As my son spends alternate weeks with his father, if I was in contact with the entire world, he would have a far greater chance to pass on the virus to his pregnant step-mum. Minuscule yes, but now on the higher end of the minuscule range.

I totally, absolutely got it. When I was pregnant, my risk register did not include an entry titled 'deadly virus'. I'm near positive, two months ago hers didn't either.

To say I was totally calm when I was carrying a baby would be a fib and I didn't even have these kinds of circumstances to panic about. Hopelessly I knew there was little I could do to take the fear away for her. There was one thing I could do. It is not only her and the baby of course. My son and his father were bathing themselves regularly in alcohol solutions and didn't dare go to the park. I get that too. The consequences of complacency could be unfathomable.

Doing the math made it clear. A circle of four or the entire damned world. You see, my boyfriend had a son, and then follows his ex-partner, her new partner, his children, their mother, her new partner and their children. Add in everyone they encounter in person and those people at the checkouts. Plus, the petrol pump handle and the delivery of takeaway. I don't even know if any of them are essential workers. I couldn't keep count. There was a pretty clear winner. And it wasn't my romantic life.

No one forced me or coerced me, it was my choice. My son and his other family versus the comfort of my fairly new lover. I planned all the FaceTime calls and emails and text messages it might take to be there for my boyfriend through whatever and whenever believing he would understand. In my risk assessment however, I did not consider those things really aren't his thing. He wanted to touch me. There goes my primary mitigation strategy out the window.

Then, after six weeks in isolation, the most magnificently confounding thing occurred.

Every morning I join a friend online for a study session. A type of accountability buddy that keeps us both on track. Although, to be fair, some mornings it's more getting off track with other conversations. This particular morning, we had cued up a Tony Robbins clip ready for his words of wisdom.

Just as we hit play, my phone rang. It was my son, who's now 11, calling from his father's house. I expected him to complain he wanted to come over to be with me for the day. He did in fact want to, but it was because his step mum was in labour.

I gave a little scream of excitement and he hung up in my ear. Apparently, I had been far too loud. I quickly called his dad, who was calm and reported the contractions had been happening since 3 a.m. The hospital had advised them to come down in an hour.

Now we three, my ex, his new wife and I, all get along extremely well. Naturally there have been all the divorce and remarrying dramas and emotions between him and me. I would not really name it friendship

Miracle #2

or love, it's just its own thing. We fight and hang up sometimes. We spend Christmas together as a family.

Until now we had managed the lockdown restrictions as a double household family well. With the baby due soon, for over a month the three of us and our son have been isolating from everyone else. My frustrated boyfriend was locked out. We'd all been eagerly awaiting the arrival of the bub and the strict isolation was a bit tough but never questioned, for safety.

As the due date was still five days away, and this being her first baby, I was a little surprised to hear the events had started but not totally shocked as my son was a week early too. I thought it diplomatic to wait until they had gone to the hospital before driving over to pick up my son.

An hour and ten minutes later I was greeted in the driveway by my son wearing a stunned mullet look in his face.

"The baby's coming," he announced. Well yes, I knew that. Then I noticed the car was still in the garage. He usually has his things ready to go but seemed to be wandering around aimlessly. He couldn't direct me as to what to do and I could sense now they were not just sitting around waiting for things to heat up.

I encouraged my son back upstairs so I could check everything was alright. I knew things had escalated when my ex came running down the stairs with a knife and covered in goop.

"She just popped it out," he proclaimed, smiling ear to ear.

In my former husband's retelling of the story to our son and me later in the evening at my house, he laughed at the moment the colour drained from my face on the stairs when he told me the baby was out!

I had eloquently exclaimed "WTF!", without the acronym.

The paramedics arrived to attend to the superwoman and the baby who I had confirmed were both perfectly okay.

I sat down with my son on the couch to keep him company. He had been waiting on that couch for the last two hours listening to the "screaming and swearing". He rushed to their assistance as directed by his father collecting pillows, then towels, then a big zip lock bag.

His dad came back out tightly snuggling a fluffy grey blanket with a pale blue beanie and a squirming, slightly purple mini person. A boy. A brother. Another son.

When I got up that morning, I had been okay in the knowledge I had moved through the grief of not having any more children and the grief for the siblings I would never give my only child. I had already wept at the thought of husband #2 having more children without me. I had let go of the feeling of loss for those parts of my body now lost to endometriosis.

I felt resolved that the arrival of this person in my son's life would outweigh any lingering jealousy and self-pity.

I was oblivious to what it might be like to witness my son meeting his newborn brother, held in my former husband's arms, minutes after he was born.

I had not considered on that day of all days as part of our disjointed and forever connected family unit, I would be there amongst it all. In the midst of it all, my ex maintained concern for me asking as he rushed around, "Are you okay? I'm sorry if this is awkward…Thank you so much for your help. Do you need to go? We don't want you to go."

When they left for the hospital, I took my son to buy flowers. He picked out a soft fawn teddy bear for his little brother.

Miracle #2

When we arrived back at home, full of adrenaline I called one friend or family member after another. All day I found myself working to resist doing the Facebook post I had written in my head. I was desperate to share this magnificent story. Apparently, the new mum laughed out loud when I messaged to say I have rightly or wrongly crowned myself Aunty Fran.

That night after my ex left his new wife and baby resting happily in the care of the nurses, he came to visit his first born. He wanted to check how he was doing after this potentially traumatic introduction to childbirth. We lapsed into stories of the day our son had been delivered into this world.

My former husband reiterated his appreciation and concern for our son and me. I realised how much we had given him on this most magical day. The things he did not have the day our son was born. Familiarity, comfort, support, calmness, people who shared in the experience too.

How opposite it had been from my experience. Two days of ongoing pre-labour pain, an emergency c-section. The nurse had sent him away soon after we arrived at the hospital in the morning, saying I was still hours away. He found himself a newspaper and ordered a hot breakfast just as the nurse called him back to join me in surgery, almost missing the excitement.

Throughout the day of his second son's birth, we shared messages and videos. The gorgeous baby was feeding eagerly. He had a long cone head and thick hair. As we recalled, our little fella had not been so keen to drink, he had the most perfect round head and light wisps of hair with a little circling cowlick on his forehead and a crooked bum crack.

I doubt I would have formed this tender attachment so quickly if I had not gone over to their house when I did. I won something unimaginable, never having foreseen the possibility of it. Most outstanding to me is knowing my son has another person in the world. For all of us the world just got bigger.

For the coming weeks the group chat photos were circulated; images of my son in the bath and the shower holding his baby brother. They melted my heart at once. Things were steadily deteriorating with my relationship and I became ever aware of my lack of connection. My endocrine system flared up, hard sore glands, headache and lethargy. Until one day the tears came. They fell hard for a full day and I was questioning everything. I sobbed, full of selfpity, over a zoom call with my boyfriend and then another zoom call with a girlfriend. Eventually I was done with it and back to my excitement as doting Aunty Fran.

CHAPTER 14

My First Sober Breakup

It was only two months after leaving my third husband for the two hundredth and final time when a man I vaguely knew asked me to his house for dinner. In typical fashion he decided I could be a keeper and we started dating. On paper and holding hands in the street we looked like an ideal couple.

A few months into this new relationship we went to a film. A regular occurrence for us. I had initially burked at the trailer to this horrific drama. His disappointment had convinced me to try even though he didn't ask me to. I ignored my inner wisdom and apprehensively went. It was set in the bushland near where I live. Filled with magnificent scenery, it was a tale of violence and revenge. A tale too close to history to pass off as fiction. I braced myself, not nearly enough. A few moments in my instinct was to run. The cinema full of people trapped me with potential embarrassment. Not wanting to make a fuss I stayed planted in my seat. When the credits rolled, I noticed my joints had seized up. I could smell the sweat of my armpits despite feeling cold. I had not moved once for the past hour yet continually shivered. As I stood I couldn't speak. I listened with horror as people casually spoke around me.

The lights of the foyer were so bright and in the ladies' room I caught sight of my white face. Others tried to make eye contact. I tried to hide. The group surrounding my boyfriend were jovial and laughing. Plans were being made to go to the pub. I slid out into the street finding the dark. Before I knew it, I was walking the hour home. Abandoning my car. Running from my boyfriend. He phoned. I couldn't answer.

Logically I knew they were actors doing a fine job. The story was written in someone's office by people who lived 150 years on. To me it felt real. It took little imagination to be there in time. How could the other movie goers talk like nothing had happened? How can it be we are so desensitised we can witness what we just saw and then go on to the pub?

With my senses on alert I could have walked all night. I needed to burn off the energy. I swung by the shop and downed a Mars bar to quell the effects of the shock. I eventually agreed to go back to my car and take my stranded boyfriend home. By the time I reached him I had stopped shaking somewhat. Honestly though, I should not have driven. Travelling in silence, he looked out the window. Halfway home the tears wouldn't wait. The snot ran from my nose. When we arrived at his house I apologised and couldn't go in. I needed my shower, my bed and my cats. I didn't sleep much as expected. My body aching as the adrenaline was processed. My mind made sure, I relived the story.

Awake at 5 a.m. the next morning, I was embarrassed and proud, not of ignoring my intuition, but for taking care of myself. This was not the first time this scene had played out. Far from it. Walking, sugar, silence, darkness, being alone, getting home, crying, cuddling my cats and a bath or a shower – these things work. Drinking, pain killers, sleeping tablets, crying in public, yelling, binging and breaking things – these are not so good. The next day I need to find something to laugh at and not make any big decisions. I will go to the park, eat something energy dense and go to bed early serving to reduce these anxiety hangover effects.

At these times I feel apart from the crowd. It's isolating to be with others who don't have the dread. To feel an invisible grasp take hold. I haven't figured out where this collective pain comes from. Is it my own experiences or that of my ancestors before me? When you know something feels odd it is people who've experienced it who can provide you support.

Even the best courses I've done, books I have read and therapists I have consulted can't explain it all. It is hard work. It is a lifetime of experimenting. Getting it right and getting it wrong. Being powerful and free in a moment. And less so in others.

The first time I tried to break up with this guy, I had a lot going on with work and life. It seemed familiar and all too overwhelming. I didn't know whether it was my job or him I needed to break up with. In the moment when I decided I needed to end it, what actually came out of my mouth as I looked at him was, "I love you". Whoops. I'm not quite sure what I thought I was doing. I didn't really know where it left me. Except work was the thing to have to go now. Wrestling with the decision to make yet another move from a job I considered what options I had. About a week later I woke up in the morning with the clarity of what I was going to do. I rang my girlfriend early in the morning and said, "Would you think I was mad if I left my job to write a book?" It is a rare and beautiful friend who encourages you no end no matter what new plan you have today.

I'm not sure I can recall breakup attempts number one, two or three but attempt number four was when we were having a weekend away. It came out on the drive down there so it was a pretty rotten weekend. Disappointed, we made the most of it and by the end of the weekend the breakup was off. All the promises of things changing didn't really help to make up for the fact our natures were too different. I endeavoured to strategise ways of being that would help us. I shared various aspects of my learnings from the professional and personal development I have undertaken. Again, that wasn't his thing.

Breakup number four, the final attempt, took a few days to play out but in the end I got there. I was waiting for the perfect ending, a way to complete what we had and finish on a good note. Something without the drama, something without the upset in anger to leave us in a good place. Something adult, bearing in mind the size of my town and having yet another ex I would no doubt have to contend with.

It has been a pattern for me when I have a breakup to return to the person in an illfated attempt to give it a second, third or fourth go. In some ways it felt like the fairer thing to do, the nice thing to do and avoid being the bad guy. When I had these other attempts to leave him I hadn't told anybody. I knew it left me space to back out and not lose any face. I had avoided the judgement of friends telling me "If I'm at that place I really just need to end it". So, this time, in contrast to every other partner I've broken up with, I made it a priority to talk to as many friends as I could the next day.

I attempted to have a laugh and remember life wouldn't be so bad without a man. I have had no more than approximately three months of being alone since I was fourteen.

In perfect synchronicity my girlfriend had just cancelled a booking at a secluded beach front property on the coast that morning. Of all my favourite places in the world this sounded like it could be one of them. I knew I needed it. If I didn't go away, I probably would have

My First Sober Breakup

gone back to him, it was my M.O. I rang the owner straight away and didn't get through. Maybe that's a sign for this isn't going to happen. Two minutes later she rang me back excited I could take the booking. I went online and paid for the house five minutes later. I'd made my commitment and looked forward to reporting back to my friend how luxurious the weekend had been.

I started to plan all the things I would take: the books and puzzles, the Netflix shows I could get through with the free wi-fi, rainforest and beaches where I could get out my camera. There wasn't any booze. It had been almost a year since the moment I quit for good. No smokes. No photos of the ex. Right on cue my phone had died. I asked the woman who set up my new one not to transfer any of the 13,000 images I had stored on the old one (not all of him, mostly cats if I'm honest). All that was left was to unfriend him on Facebook. I rang another friend and asked her to feed the cats and promised to catch up next week.

I texted another friend. I had one night before I went away so we arranged to watch a movie instead of me ending up in bed with you know who again. I think the structure saved me. It only took 10 minutes of planning when I got out of my way and asked people for help. Funny how it's so hard to take them up on the offer. I wonder if that stopped them from asking me to do the same for them?

My son has been around for these various relationships. Some of the situations have been hard on him and I work with my guilt. We talk about what he wants to do and the parts he understands. I hope he talks to his therapist about the part he doesn't understand when he's older.

I promised my son it was over. I asked him how he felt about it. He said he didn't know. Something tells me he did. In our new house, he and I have a new safety. He often doesn't want to go anywhere else. At night we watch silly comedies and laugh at things I don't think he actually understands. After watching a particularly interesting episode one night I decided to give his father a call and suggested he have a bit of a talk. Time to build on what he already knows about growing up.

He had mentioned to me one of the boys has been looking up things on his phone down on the school oval through the day where there is very little supervision from the duty teachers. I think he's at the stage where he just walked away feeling disgusted adults would do such things. He told me he had a terrible week because the table he was assigned to for the fortnight was him and three girls. The quiet one, the sassy one and the smelly one. I don't think I've got too much to worry about just yet. I knew after the time he and I had lived with my third husband, I wouldn't possibly move him into a house with another man. This played on my mind in my new relationship. I suppose it's human nature to fantasise about the possibilities in a relationship. Knocking this option out left me feeling disillusioned about our relationship in the future.

The weeks my new boyfriend and I had our children, it was all parental responsibility, school runs, soccer practice, tennis classes and super marketing for lunch supplies. The boys were different ages and different stages and apart from the iPad they had very little in common. In fact, they didn't even agree on what they were going to do on the iPad. On the weeks the boys were with our respective partners we had an opportunity to do all kinds of adult things. We would go out for lovely meals, stay in for lovely meals, watch movies, go to the cinema, take weekend trips away together, walk on the beach and of course do it at every opportunity. This felt like the similar disjointed life with husband #3. It felt disconnected.

I was seeking authenticity and support to grow, to build a magnificent life. In the end, worry and anxiety about other aspects of our relationship combined with this sense of discombobulation got all a bit too much.

Despite my progress in self-development, I found the breakup a wonderful opportunity for me to dive back into obsessive things. It was necessary to revamp my wardrobe, kind of like a Marie Kondo system. I look at each piece then everything with a huge attachment goes out with the man. A costume I wore to a fun dress up party together, a formal dress from a significant event or a bikini once worn on a seaside holiday. The purging includes jewellery if it was a gift, but I draw the line at shoes.

Now, the empty coat hangers call to be filled so the shopping compulsion is justified. A new look, a new me, a new way to look in the world. Op shops have really profited from my man cycling over the years.

Having a new freedom from prior food and alcohol compulsions, the shopping is the one of three tactics usually employed left. Seems like a step forward.

The final piece of the puzzle is usually the hair. From long to short, from blonde to brunette, to red. This time I discussed my options with my son. He confirmed his preference for the current blonde and when questioned what he thought about me cutting it to my shoulders he answered, "No because you wouldn't be you."

I was busy planning and hustling with shopping sprees to be the next version of me. He validated in that moment, he wanted me to be the me he already had.

I was curious we both assigned my physical appearance to who I am. I know better, yet it was still there. This was my chance to demonstrate to him I am who I am either way. I can be fun and serious, loving and responsible in exactly the same way with hot pink ringlets bouncing above my shoulders. I come from my way of being fabulous. External glam is optional.

CHAPTER 15

Guaranteed Destruction

One day it will all be answered. All fixed and solved. This beautiful story will be complete, and I will be gone. Forever left only to be alive in the thoughts and lives of others.

Now, in a little seaside cottage sitting by a blazing fire in my Ugg boots I have an ending for my story. Not for my whole story, just the one so far. I look forward to writing a sequel when I'm 80 and then complete a trilogy at 120. Maybe I could compile a few chapters in between just in case I don't make it that far.

I wonder what words I will have left in my filled journals. The difference now is I really don't mind who finds them, I'm pretty sure they'll be tossed out with the balance of my accumulated existence and debris only ever precious to me.

Graced with Womanhood

We are all time bombs without the visible clock in most cases. We are certainly equipped with a mechanism for self-destruction and at risk of accidental detonation. If I am a time bomb why shouldn't I be a dancing one? There is no way to know my scheduled explosion day. So why not get jiggy and carry on like it's eons away.

For my sequel memoir to be titled '*How to be Fabulous*', I do hope it doesn't feature another series of divorces, my career wifing must end! I'd also prefer it is free from addictions, violence, obsessions, and general major shittiness. I concede there is likely to be some perhaps unlovable parts, I have no idea what is to come.

Right now, waiting for sunrise there's a promise of excitement in the moment. The dark sky revealed lighter shades and hues of yellow, pink and blue. I wonder if this morning dawn will differ from yesterday. What will it bring to me in the hours ahead? As the brightest edge crests across the horizon, whether over the sea in the west or mountains in the east, an air of possibility breaks. My day may have already started with a simple hour of writing, providing the sense of achievement even if nothing else is accomplished that day.

Whatever occurs for me, whatever happens, I was present in it from the starting. Ageing has had that effect on me. Every morning a tiny voice way back of my mind wonders, if this is to be the last rising of the sun I am to see. The speed at which the planet spins appears phenomenal in this moment as the glaring sphere rises from almost nowhere. No matter how cold the air is, the warmth is instantly radiated with the arrival of the gassy giant.

If I'm lucky, the moon will be visible on the horizon simultaneously. A new moon doubling the prospect of hope in my heart. Of course, I dare not look at Sol directly, but Lunar allows my eyes to rest, the distance relaxing the muscles used mostly to focus on nearby objects.

Guaranteed Destruction

The full moon is illuminated so brightly, it allows for my attention far longer than the present vision of the sun. First, I tried to figure out when each dark patch was made, musing at my incomprehension at how long ago each impact of flying objects collided so far away.

I think proudly of my star sign. My amusing attention to the Zodiac started as a fantasy of connection years ago. The alignment of the moon being both funny and comforting. Despite its seeming ridiculousness to the rational, if it lends me something, what harm must it do. Too many times I've experienced synchronicity to my future told through the stars. Too often its sentiments align with what's on my mind. I really don't know if I believe any of it actually but playing with its potential to be relevant is interesting if nothing else. I think it speaks to the hope I have for life.

Today could be occupied with busy periods of frenzied work or relaxed and playful times. Perhaps partly both. Undoubtedly, I'll forget how the morning broke and I don't pay the glorious sight much more attention.

As the afternoon brightness drops and the air changes its feel, the evening slowly takes over from the day's meteorology. I try to be aware of this change in preparation for the sunset. I aim to take the second opportunity to spy Lunar flying around us and watch another goodbye to Sol.

There are more tragedies that happened in every single one of these days than my soul can bear to think of. The time it takes for the sun to disappear again brings with it, countless more today. If I manage to step away from the task I'm engaged in long enough to say goodbye I bring my awareness to this reality.

I wonder who is watching this same scene. Friends and family scattered around the world, most of whom may not have featured in my day. Their experience will be at different times in the universe, slightly upside down to me. I consider former loves maybe also looking up at this vision. I wonder if any of them think of me at the same moment I remembered them.

I was having a text conversation with a good friend to update her on my extended time at the beach. She asked how I was coping with the breakup and I reported my uplifting surroundings were doing wonders. She was both jealous and happy for me like any true friend would be.

We laughed, joking about our romantic prospects or lack thereof. I confided I had taken action to lessen my depression by ordering a new personal toy online. She lamented she had recently thrown out her naughty box in fear her teenage kids would find it if she died. I told her I thought they would understand, if not now, when they are older.

Seems we all fear others discovering particular aspects of ourselves and the real women we are. Time to do something about that.

When I arrived home from my beach tranquillity, my present to myself had arrived by express post. Did they hear desperation on my order form? I was relieved my son wasn't home, he has a habit of excitedly opening my deliveries in the hope they are for him. Not this time buddy.

I told my girlfriend I'd give her a review in a couple of weeks. Now I have the perfect gift idea for her.

PART II

For the Love of Womanhood

I grappled with writing this section. It seems I am surrounded by so many experts, maturity and distinguished people. I wrestled with my desire to share a humble contribution to what in life has challenged and continues to transform me.

There was a time I prided myself on having an open mind and heart, a growth mindset and a non-judgmental outlook on the world and its inhabitants. I have since realised in this matter I was deluding myself somewhat. Instead, I would admit to being curious about many things and vaguely interested in others. It's a less noble and profound realisation and that's okay.

I found out it was okay to not really understand who I was and to be scared to get to know myself.

Graced with Womanhood

I accept it is perfectly natural to be overwhelmed by how the universe is playing out and the stupid things people do both big and small.

Turns out not many topics are off limits in this book and this next section is no different. You've seen how these tales have unfolded, now let us change tack. This next part is less story and more how I have grown to flourish, playing this animated game of living.

We are born into a world with a universal conversation and an inherited nature. Much of which is taken for granted now did not exist ten, twenty or a thousand years ago and may not exist in the years to come.

My hard fought and modest amount of wisdom did not appear to me by chance or with wonder. It grew from lesson after lesson, from trying over and over again. Three marriages might attest to perseverance or one of those stupid things people do. No matter either way.

I am convinced we advocate for and mentor each other in this wondrously crazy existence. The following pages contain some of the choice contributions I have gathered. I ask you to consider where the women who share your life would value your wisdom.

After all, we know what we know when we know it and when we know more, we are capable of more.

> *"I like living. I have sometimes been wildly, despairingly, acutely miserable, racked with sorrow, but through it all I still know quite certainly that just to be alive is a grand thing."*
> **Agatha Christie**

Can we agree there is still stigma around mental health and its treatment? For me, so much anxiety and depression continued to manifest after being diagnosed with anxiety and depression.

I believe the best advocate for me is me. Professional help is vital, and heaven knows I've had my fair share. I will add, it was vital when I was ready. Being willing and motivated increased my presence in every part of the treatment.

Doctor Google has its traps, however, being prepared and aware of the language was super helpful. Asking questions and then asking again also made a big difference to the empowerment I had in the process and the results.

Pumps, foils, capris, gel tips, ink, mascara, straightness, cammies, belly studs, hosiery, toner, blush, razor cuts, laser, acrylics, falsies, brazilians, concealer, push-ups, stilettos, chicken fillets, tape, g-strings, wedges, teddies, peels, Cedel, fascinators, slips, maxies, halters, sponges, diamenties, shellac and bronzer.

I wish I could say this is an exhaustive list, but all I can say is that I was exhausted just writing it. These are a few things I have bought and paid for over the years, some year in and year out. As you may imagine it's not only physically exhausting, acquiring them all is mentally and financially exhausting too. Imagine if I kept going with this list? No actually don't.

My relationship to my body as an object has had an exhausting impact on my quality of life. I know very few women who haven't struggled in some way to love the bag of meat carrying their soul around. Modern cultural stigma is all encompassing, it envelops our self-image well before we have cognition it's happened. It is all relative, at the time I did not know any different.

Without respect for my body as it is, I was unable to look past comparisons made to an illusionary vision around me. Dieting and endless cycling around weight and wellness steals time and in essence, life. The evolution of beauty standards and sexualisation soaks womankind in fantasy and a version of insanity. It is a multi-billion-dollar industry that would dry up overnight if everyone said, "I'm enough exactly as I am." Yet it persists.

From body dysmorphia to disordered eating to obsessive compulsive behaviours to risky sexy business I walked along in this universe trying desperately to crack the code.

When I got married, each time, the whole production was as you can expect, mind bending planning and scheduling for perfection. I had painful laser treatment, excruciating scrapping and acid peels and light therapy brighter than the sun. All to disappear blemished and leave 'naturally' beautiful skin. All to be buried under lashings of makeup applied by skilled artists.

For my 40th birthday I sprung for a boudoir shoot in Sydney. I was super excited about rocking my bod in stilettos and nothing else. It was incredible fun and yet I didn't feel like Wonderwoman as anticipated. I'd been naked in front of women before, had my photo taken before and been made up like a Western Geisha before too. Funnily enough I didn't have as much to prove to myself as I thought. When I look at the album now who I see is so far from the daily me no one would recognise me. Only my green eyes. I've never tried to change them and think they are the best part of me.

It took work to find alternative ways out and there are plenty out there to find. The body acceptance movement is growing and doing a fabulous job to educate and support everyone, including women.

Be assured I still wear makeup and try to find clothes I reckon look alright. I do not expect to wash off 42 years of creation immediately. It's happening as I look for new information, try on new perspectives rather than expecting to find peace in a new pair of jeans.

For the Love of Womanhood

My point is, even when I go into full body worship mode the satisfaction is fleeting, if at all. All the worry and prep work doesn't mean anything greater is available to me in my life and overall has the nasty habit of consuming more than it nourishes.

Ultimately, as we've all been told so many times, it's not how the world sees you that matters, it's how you see yourself. I had to learn to stop looking through other peoples' eyes.

Of all the gorgeous humans I've known, one friend dropped to her kitchen floor and died of a brain aneurysm with her two children under five in the house. Another friend chose to complete a pregnancy, forgoing treatment for cervical cancer, soon after the birth she lost her life. Another mate had a rare blood cancer. For many years he struggled to manage. Eventually he left behind his wife and three teenage children.

Another friend meticulously planned his death to provide for the life of his former wife and two small children in the years to come. Another died in his bed in his early 30s having experienced his entire adult life with alcoholism. His mother died two years beforehand from breast cancer. Another gorgeous lady with a love for parties recently succumbed to ovarian cancer.

My beloved Grandfather had a turn in his armchair on Christmas in his armchair in front of my Grandma, Mum, Dad, brother and me. He went into a nursing home and didn't speak again before he passed away. My Nan died of lung cancer, it was my Pop, her husband who smoked. He died shortly afterwards as is often the case. My Granny died at 96. She was my namesake and one of my favourite people ever.

My first memory of death occurred at age six when my Mum's niece lost her child who was new to walking. He wandered away from his grandparent's and into a damn covered in lily pads.

I am certain you will have a collection of these happenings in your experience of life too. I point to this as a reminder, and for some a hidden consciousness, of how precious life is. I am humbled to have been present to others who have been with death and travel with it freely.

I consider my mortality every single day. I was once scared of the ruminating, seeing it as a dark preoccupation. Now I can say clearly, I cling to my awareness as a reality check to every day, every hour and every minute. In all realms of life, I ask, "If not now, when?"

"When you touch other people, when your words impact them and your actions empower them, your life has both meaning and purpose."

Marissa Peer

Of all the joy in my life many of my most beloved memories contain others. Not always the days at the beach or on rides at Disneyland or my not-so-surprise birthday parties but the times I was stretched and broken and people were there. Those moments when I asked for help and it was extended with love and compassion.

I've done a lot of reading and asked a lot of questions about relating to people. My conclusion thus far; I can't save them or fix them or change them one little bit, but I can be there. The space for listening is a most precious gift.

I've been told by partners, "You make me want to be a better man." Maybe they all saw it in some pivotal movie during their adolescence? However, I think the sentiment highlights 'want to' and that's not the same as 'am being'. I get this sounds like it's not me, it's them. That's to say; it's not up to me, it's not even possible for me to make anyone a better version of themselves. They are in charge of all their actions. I am only in charge of mine.

For the Love of Womanhood

Sex, hey. Wow it's fun. Really fun, or it can be. It can be wondrous, amazing exciting beautiful and downright spiritual. It can be with one person or more, same sex or not, it can be awful, painful, disappointing, a chore, a duty, unwanted or unwelcome. It can be illegal, or so in my experience.

All that said, I advocate for far more education. My experience of school sex education was the drawing on the blackboard of a cow looking representation of the female anatomy by my extremely nervous male grade 5 teacher who then proceeded to drown a tampon in a beaker of water. I got the message of what goes where and you shouldn't really do it but not a lot of it could go this way or that way or around this other way and everything could be amazing.

What can I say about pop culture? It takes five minutes of contemplation to get honest with the influence it has on us. For me still. The whole world of sexuality is fraught with its impact. Stepping out of what is so conveniently put in front of me was hard. For example, I had not ever considered the existence of ethical porn. It might not be easy to find or live up to the normal type we are used to experiencing. It is however an encouraging way forward.

When you're in the middle of a situation involving violence and abuse it can be harder to recognise than you realise.

"Why don't they just leave?" I've heard so many bloody times. How is that helpful?

It may not be obvious how to respond to friends and family, any human being who is experiencing abuse. Even though your spider sense may tingle you may not know if you need to call an ambulance or the police and in a moment of indecision, in my humble opinion, act. What's the worst that can happen? Something worse might happen if you don't.

Reasons why people stay? They don't want to sleep in the car, they believe it will change, they don't have access to money, they don't want to uproot or traumatise their children, they're afraid they'll lose their children. They're doing the best they can in the midst of a fog of anxiety and depression. They don't have access to help. They don't want to admit to anyone it's happening. They don't know it's happening. They're afraid for their lives and that of their children.

It is very real that people manage to manipulate and deceive others into believing, truly believing, it's all them. Exhausted and confused they feel they are in the wrong, they are the cause of all the problems, and take on responsibility.

I've had friends ring in the middle of trauma when I was on a date in a restaurant, at midnight when I was sound asleep and when I've been in my office working away. With the distance between us all I had the power to do was listen. Listen and consider the actions available to me. Do I give them advice, could I refer them to services, or should I get in the car and go be with them? In the end the most common action required was to listen. If action is needed again, I say act.

Many people who leave a situation also go back. It didn't last because they weren't convinced. We need to do these things in our own time. The power can come in time. If any of this is speaking to you, please know you are doing the best you can at any moment and people will help you if you ask.

Self love. I'm talking about getting to know and appreciate the whole of you. The worrying messed up and confused you. I find analysing my thoughts and behaviour and considering my strengths and weaknesses can generate internal jostling. It's amusing and sometimes fun but mostly it helps to see where I'm coming from.

Nothing is foolproof, and you probably won't unravel your purpose or source of being, but honestly would you want to? So what I'm suggesting is some of the tried and partly true methods out there, those behavioural tools and education have something to offer. Just as I cautioned with every other suggestion I have made, please take what works, transform what doesn't and throw the rest out.

I say give yourself love. What I want for you is to be compassionate with yourself. Give empathy to yourself before you spread it around. Some of the options for personal growth may spark a realisation about your life or that of others within it. You can put as much effort in as you fancy, and you might find yourself fascinated if you do a little work.

I applied for a leadership programme when I was 31. On the application I was asked what my values were. To be candid I had no flipping clue. I'm pretty sure I went online and Googled personal values and picked a few I thought would be what they wanted to hear. Sounds pretty lame now of course but I give myself some slack because no one had ever asked me before.

So maybe you've never thought about it either or maybe a quick refresh is in order. There also might be a younger person who would benefit from you posing these types of questions. This vocation can be as deep as you make it.

May I suggest you also do a simple exercise by reviewing a list of values online too. At least consider if your actions are living up to the values you are instantly attracted to. A word of caution, you are what you say you are and you can say whatever you want.

I crafted the words in the first section of this book to share a truth for myself with no ultimate meaning. It was with sadness and love I managed the retelling. It was with joy and inspiration I formed a possible future for myself and those who join me in life.

I have not intended, at any point, to embarrass or shame anybody who has been in my life and features in snippets of this book. As characters in my world I bring them to life in my storytelling. It happens the world over and has for all of history.

To be free with expressing myself I have shared what happened to me and how I experienced those events. My peace and forgiveness of self has enabled me to take value in all of it. This is in contrast to gossip and I trust you will treat my authenticity and vulnerability with respect. I deeply acknowledge the contribution all these people have made to my life.

I would wholeheartedly recommend writing your own memoir, in part or completely. Anyone can do it; it doesn't have to be wonderful to anyone other than you. Heaven knows I clung to that thought as I wrote.

Whatever your motivation I promise you discoveries will open up and then you'll have the option to do whatever you choose to do with them. Hold on to them, make a book or give them away. You don't need to share it with everyone, you also might want to share it with at least one someone.

Some days I hold as perfect memories and writing about those days keeps them alive. This story is an example of the latter.

With cupped hands my son held the creature gently. The butterfly's interruption was unexpected. We all stopped to take it in. It clung to

For the Love of Womanhood

him softly giving us a moment to contemplate its being. We were puzzled at its blue spots and beady eyes. A winged reminder beauty and wonder drops by unannounced.

My son is very practiced at holding still for a camera. The true magic of the moment was fleeting. The other prize is this digital memory. Animate or inanimate, I look first through my naked eyes and then through the lens. There is more for me to see from this perspective. Adding curiosity and compassion.

Surrounded by art from many cultures, I treasure creating some for myself. I gave up drawing and storytelling just like I gave up childhood. With some good luck and coaching I have come back to these joys.

I work to my own inspirations as I am creating. At times it is fun and uplifting. Other times it's cruelly frustrating. Whatever the outcome, when I am done there's peace. It's not always good and it's often not great, but it's mine. It probably doesn't look like the image in my mind yet it's just perfect as it is.

Elizabeth Gilbert wrote "art does not have to be important or save the world." I checked and today there's 7.770ish billion people here with me. So that's probably just as well. My photos and paintings won't save any of them. Almost all of them won't see any of it. Though if I'm bold a few might. They're certainly not important. They are only slightly so to me. Yet I love it, I really do. For years outlets of creativity usually gave way to sensible things like being an accountant and paying my bills.

Gilbert writes of courage and persistence in living a creative life. Her soothing reassurances left me eager to explore. She speaks of enchantment and divinity. I worked with productivity and flow, of being in "the zone". These are all concepts and are true, if they are true for us. The romantic ideal was far more attractive.

I reminisce and renew my childhood creative energy. Recalling times I have lost myself in a project. The books spread over the kitchen table, the pallets of wet paint piled up in the sink. Running down the street, barefoot on the bitumen to get the power lines out of my sunset shot before the sun disappears.

One tropical island snorkelling trip ended without any dignity as I crawled up the beach on all fours in my bikini dry retching. I spent way too long underwater being swept back and forth by the current, holding the rope on the boat's anchor, trying to get *the* shot, amidst a school of fish.

Creativity for me looks like photography, writing, painting in acrylic, watercolors and pastels. As well as hand lettering and calligraphy, sketch note drawings, needle work and building miniature models. I recently made a chance decision to join a painting class. There are four other gals who have different approaches. It was daunting to walk in the first day, our easels set up in the centre of a studio, the walls covered with paintings for sale. Over the weeks those paintings revealed all kinds of colours and shapes. I see light and shade everywhere in life in a whole new way. I look deeper now at the skyline and moon at night.

I am a big fan of expressive therapy, whether it be something including singing, dancing, drawing, working with clay or collaging for example. I would highly recommend giving it a go. Could a road out of suffering be play? That's got to excite some of you. Creative pursuits energetically generate the power and freedom to come out in the world inside a new personal reality. It's saved me from myself time and time again. I'd love for you to have these experiences for yourself however they may be.

Afterword

If you ever start to think you are not enough give me a call. I will happily remind you, you are. When I am in wonder of creation, I have access to joy, love and oneness. And you, you are a wonder of creation.

I've decided to live as if I'm sticking around. If there is somewhere else to be it can remain a mystery for now. I could have as many years of life again before it is completed, or tomorrow might be it. I could have a hundred more years and what a thought that is.

I believe we have evolved from primal mammals. That's not to say I am discounting anyone's belief; we continue to evolve either way. Homo sapiens have demonstrated we are violent and self-interested, kind and benevolent. We continue to live in harsh unsophisticated circumstances and in luxury and complex social structures.

We are contrasted in nature and actions yet made of the same parts and components. I am at peace with this in some moments and in others I would rather not be in this version of the universe.

Graced with Womanhood

While I am here, conscious and able, I look to the wonder and beauty in the world. The joys extended in the universe console my distressed mind and body. On my better days anyway.

For me, the wonder in the world is enough.

Further Reading

10 Billion by Stephen Emmott

50 Philosophy Ideas You Really Need to Know by Ben Dupre

A Very Short History of the World by Geoffrey Blainey

All I Need to Know I Learned from My Cat by Suzy Becker

Allness in Heart www.allnessinheart.com

Anti-Diet: Reclaim your time, money, well-being and happiness through Intuitive Eating by Christy Harrison

Beauty Redefined: www.beautyredefined.org

Better than Before by Gretchen Rubin

Big Magic by Elizabeth Gilbert

Brave Enough by Cheryl Strand

Creative Live www.creativelive.com

Curable www.curablehealth.com

Graced with Womanhood

Dangerous Woman by Clare Conville, Liz Hoggard & Sarah-Jane Lovett Dare to Lead by Brene Brown

Dieting Causes Brain Damage by Bradley Trevor

Grieve by Ellen Shuman www.aweighout.com

Emotional Freedom Technique www.dailyom.com

Feel the Fear and Do It Anyway by Susan Jeffery

Fight Like a Girl by Clementine Ford

Get Out of Your Mind and Into Your Life: The New Acceptance and Commitment Therapy by Steven C. Hayes & Spencer Smith

Get Your Shit Together by Sarah Knight

Goodreads www.goodreads.com *Guardians of Being* by Eckart Tolle

Health at Every Size by Linda Bacon

1800RESCT www.1800respect.org.au

Our Watch www.ourwatch.org.au

Ideapod: ideapod.com

Intuitive Eating by Elyse Resch & Evelyn Tribole

Jay Shetty www.jayshetty.me

Landmark Insights by Landmark Worldwide Landmark: www.landmarkworldwide.com

Lifeline www.lifeline.org.au

Make the Most of You by Patrick Lindsay

Man's Search for Meaning by Viktor Frankl

Marisa Peer www.marisapeer.com

Medium Blogs www.medium.com

Men at Work: Australia's Parenthood Trap (Quarterly Essay #75) by Annabel Crabb

Mindfulness and Compassion by The Happy Buddha

Further Reading

Mindvalley www.mindvalley.com

On Being www.onbeing.org

Fearless Rebelle Radio Podcast

iweigh with Jameela Jamil Podcast

Protectometer by GL Moseley & DS Butler

Revolution by Russell Brand

Rising Woman www.risingwoman.com

Sapiens: A Brief History of Humankind by Yuval Noah Harari

Speaking Being by Wherner Erhard & Marting Heidegger

Stillness Speaks by Eckart Tolle Summer Innanen @summerinnanen

The Architecture of Happiness by Alain de Botton

The Art of Happiness by His Holiness the Dalai Lama & Howard Cutler

The Art of Living Alone and Loving It by Jane Mathews

The Artist's Way by Julia Cameron

The Book of Myself by Carl & David Marshall

The Consolations of Philosophy by Alain de Botton

The Easy Way for Woman to Stop Drinking by Allen Carr

The Empaths Survival Guide by Judith Orloff

The Five Love Languages by Gary Chapman

The Form of Things by A C Grayling

The Four Agreements by don Miguel Ruiz

The Fuck-it Diet Caroline Dooner

The Good Cause: www.thegoodcause.co

The Happiness Trap by Russell Harris

The Joy of Mindful Sex by Claudia Blake

The Lifted Brow Quarterly Journal

The Little Book of Philosophy by Andre Comte-Sponville

The Power of Now by Eckhart Tolle

The School of Life: www.theschooloflife.com

The Subtle Art of Not Giving a Fuck by Mark Manson

Tony Robins www.tonyrobbins.com

Ultimate 48 Hour Author www.natasadenman.com

We: A Manifesto for Women Everywhere by Gillian Anderson & Jennifer Nadel

Winnie the Pooh by A. A. Milne

Woman Kind Magazine www.womankindmag.com

About the Author

Frances Pratt was born and resides in Launceston and is well known in Tasmania with over 15 years' experience in the not-for-profit sector. She brings vigour to her varied roles with organisations and ventures she creates in action to serve the community. A mother, a CEO, a Cancerian, a cat lady and a divorcee three times over, Frances illustrates a nature of curiosity and resolve, framed by empathy.

A chartered accountant by original qualification Frances worked in the field for ten years before moving into the community services. She established a small business enterprise as a shared space for woman to launch their alternative therapy practices and work their passion projects. Frances facilitated leadership programs with an organisation dedicated to the creation of great leaders. She has worked as a massage therapist and established a pop-up boudoir photography business empowering woman to play and have fun!

Graced with Womanhood

Frances is currently the CEO of the sexual assault service in her region and has a new puppy, Luna. Frances continues to delve into growth and development projects and is exploring expressive therapies from the view of creation in joy and wonder in people's lives. Writing this book was in line with her declaration to elevate conversations and growing movements for woman in society compassionately and courageously as an evolving form of authenticity.

About the Author

About the Author

About the Author

Graced with Womanhood

Acknowledgements

I am tempted to mention every soul I have ever met and those I haven't. There are of course those who featured more prominently and impactfully in my life. To my most precious son, thank you for shredding all my drafts. I love you tirelessly. For my Mum and Dad, I now understand your lifelong dedication to my brother and I, and just how much your love in action means to me. For my awesome brother and his family, I don't tell you how much I love you anywhere near enough. For the men who love me, I hold your love with gratitude. To all my friends, best, past and furry, you give me humanity and I live so many lives sharing in yours. To the multiverse, thank you for always loving me and knowing my being is enough. Your beauty is miraculous.

www.ingramcontent.com/pod-product-compliance
Lightning Source LLC
Chambersburg PA
CBHW021441080526
44588CB00009B/626